The Enigma of Justice

The Enigma of Justice

Morris A. Inch

WIPF & STOCK · Eugene, Oregon

THE ENIGMA OF JUSTICE

Copyright © 2010 Morris A. Inch. All rights reserved. Except for brief quotations in critical publications or reviews, no part of this book may be reproduced in any manner without prior written permission from the publisher. Write: Permissions, Wipf and Stock Publishers, 199 W. 8th Ave., Suite 3, Eugene, OR 97401.

Wipf & Stock
An Imprint of Wipf and Stock Publishers
199 W. 8th Ave., Suite 3
Eugene, OR 97401
www.wipfandstock.com

ISBN 13: 978-1-60899-763-3

Manufactured in the U.S.A.

Contents

Preface / vii

Acknowledgments / ix

1. Justice and the Prophets / 1
2. Justice and the Cardinal Virtues / 11
3. Justice and the Theories / 20
4. Justice and Faith / 30
5. Justice and Hope / 38
6. Justice and Love / 46
7. Commutative Justice / 54
8. Distributive Justice / 62
9. Legal Justice / 70
10. Retributive Justice / 78
11. Justice and Poverty / 86
12. Justice and Mercy / 94
13. Justice and Freedom / 102
14. Justice and Life / 111
15. Justice and Idolatry / 119
16. Justice and Reality / 127
17. International Justice / 135
18. The Legacy / 143

Bibliography / 151

Preface

WHILE JUSTICE IS A CRITICAL COMPONENT OF CORPORATE LIFE, ITS meaning is variously understood. This not uncommonly leads to confusion, incrimination, and even conflict. It recalls an amusing story concerning a man who was accosted while crossing the property of another. "How did you come about laying claim to this land?" the intruder inquired.

"I inherited it from my father," the other confidently replied.

"And how did he come by it?" the former persisted.

"From his father, and grandfather before him," the latter acknowledged. He assumed this established his inheritance.

"But how was it originally obtained?" the intruder pressed his reluctant host.

"He fought for it!" the now irate owner exclaimed.

"I'll fight you for it!" the challenger heartily responded. This seemed to him an equitable way of proceeding.

A fanciful account? Likely so, but not all that different in principle from one who insists on preferential treatment to address some real or imaginary wrong inflicted on those of his ethnic background, gender, race, or sexual preference in the past. In this manner, it constitutes an appeal to justice.

With such in mind, we initially turn to the school of the prophets. "I hate, I despise your religious feasts, I cannot stand your assemblies," the Lord protests. "Even though you bring me burnt offerings and grain offerings, I have no regard for them. Away with the noise of your songs! I will not listen to the music of your harps" (Amos 5:21-22). Accordingly, hypocrisy compounds their guilt.

"But let justice roll on like a river, righteousness like a never-failing stream!" the Almighty subsequently admonishes his wayward people. In a region where wadis (dry river beds) proliferate, this amounts to an appeal for abundance and constancy. In this particular instance, *justice* and *righteousness* appear in parallel construction and hence more or less synonymous. Otherwise, their connotations may differ.

We shortly turn our attention to *justice* as one of the four cardinal virtues. This will further serve to establish its critical importance for society as a whole, and persons individually. Thereafter, we will consider several prominent theories concerning justice.

In turn, we will touch on justice as associated with each of the theological/spiritual virtues: faith, hope, and love. After that, consider four classical definitions: concerning commutative, distributive, legal, and retributive justice. We will then explore some of the remaining nuances of this complex subject. Finally, conclude with a discussion of the legacy of justice, as a cherished gift to subsequent generations. Consequently, it bears repeating: "But let justice roll on like a river, righteousness like a never-failing stream!"

Acknowledgments

My beloved wife Joan, took on the demanding task as copy editor for this text, having just edited *Thumbs Up For the Family*, subsequently published. It goes without saying, I am deeply appreciative.

1

Justice and The Prophets

It was the unenviable task of the prophets to fine-tune the monarchy to its covenant obligations. There was considerable room for improvement, needless to say. Accordingly, Hosea pointedly complains: "There is no faithfulness, no love, no acknowledgment of God in the land. There is only cursing, lying and murder, stealing and adultery" (4:1–2).

What sort of a person was the prophet? For one thing, he exhibited a keen sensitivity to the evil surrounding him. In this regard, "To us a single act of injustice—cheating in business, exploitation of the poor—is slight; to the prophets, a disaster. To us injustice is injurious to the welfare of the people; to the prophets it is a deathblow to existence: to us, an episode; to them, a catastrophe, a threat to the world."[1] How are we to account for this contrast between the prophets and general populace? It is as if the former were marching to a different cadence. As a result, they could better appreciate the gravity of sin—as an affront to the Almighty. Although it assuredly had social and personal implications as well.

Again, what sort of person was the prophet? He was not reluctant to challenge those in authority, when it seemed that they had lost their way. Moreover, to warn of impending disaster should they continue in their wickedness. Not only for themselves, but subsequent generations.

In contrast, "A tribal god was petitioned to slay the tribe's enemies because he was conceived as the god of that tribe and not as the god of its enemies. When the Roman armies were defeated in battle, the people,

---

1. Heschel, *The Prophets*, 8.

indignant, did not hesitate to wreck the images of their gods."[2] This is by way of reminding us that persons are no better than the deities they profess to serve.

Finally, what sort of person was the prophet? In preparation for the prophetic ministry, it might be said: "'All flattery abandon, you who enter here.' To be a prophet is both a distinction and an affliction. The mission he performs is distasteful to him and repugnant to others; no reward is promised him and no reward could temper its bitterness."[3]

Jeremiah serves as a classic example. "So the word of the Lord has brought me insult and reproach all day long," he complains. "But if I say, 'I will not mention him or speak any more in his name,' his word is in my heart like a fire, a fire shut up in my bones. I am weary of holding it in; indeed, I cannot" (Jer 20:8–9).

Justice receives little explicit mention prior to the Mosaic Covenant. As a prime exception, the Almighty reflects: "Shall I hide from Abraham what I am about to do? For I have chosen him, so that he will direct his children and his household after him to keep the way of the Lord by doing what is right and just, so that the Lord will bring about for Abraham what he has promised him" (Gen 18:17, 19).

"The point is stressed, because it is the spiritual/moral basis that enabled Abraham to intercede for the deliverance of Sodom." Moreover, "It was also on the basis of Abraham's right relationship with God that Yahweh guaranteed to deliver Lot from the coming conflagration of these cities. Furthermore, in this account Abraham, a doer of righteousness, stands in sharp relief to the doers of wickedness in Sodom."[4] This, in turn, set the course for all those who refer to the patriarch as the father of the faithful (cf. Heb 11:8–12).

Whereas Abraham epitomized the patriarchal era as no other, Moses introduced the period of the prophets. In Jewish tradition, he is remembered primarily as a rabbi/teacher, although instrumental in the deliverance of his people from bondage. In greater detail, the angel of the Lord appeared to him in the context of a burning bush that was not consumed.

---

2. Ibid., 12.
3. Ibid., 17–18.
4. Hartley, *Genesis*, 181.

When he approached the bush to observe this strange phenomenon more closely, God cautioned him: "Do not come any closer. Take off your sandals, for the place where you are standing is holy ground." Then he revealed, "I am the God of your father, the God of Abraham, the God of Isaac and the God of Jacob" (Exod 3:5–6). At this, Moses hid his face, because he was afraid to confront the Almighty.

"I have indeed seen the misery of my people in Egypt," the Lord assured him. "I have heard them crying out because of their slave drivers, and I am concerned about their suffering. So I have come down to rescue them from the hand of the Egyptians and to bring them up out of that land into a good and spacious land, a land flowing with milk and honey." In other words, to a land of plenty.

"So now, go I am sending you to Pharaoh to bring my people the Israelites out of Egypt," the Almighty continued. At this, Moses protested—in that he did not feel adequate for such a monumental task. "I will be with you," God countered. "And this will be the sign to you that it is I who have sent you. When you have brought the people out of Egypt, you will worship God on this mountain." This, moreover, recalls the observation that one with God is in the majority.

Moses was still reluctant. "Suppose I go to the Israelites and say to them, 'The God of your fathers has sent me to you,' and they ask me, 'What is his name?' Then what shall I tell them?" This was tantamount to inquiring what new revelation he had received.

"I Am Who I Am," the Lord replied. "This is what you are to say to the Israelites; 'I am has sent me to you.'" This is likely a reference to *the living Lord*, as set over against all pretenders. In this regard, "Of what value is an idol, since a man has carved it? Or an image that teaches lies? For he who makes it trusts in his own creation; he makes idols that cannot speak" (Hab 2:18).

Or, if cast in terms of the future, God's ways will become known in the course of time. Consequently, heed his injunctions with relentless confidence. As expressed by Dietrich Bonhoeffer: "Those who obey, trust; and those who trust, obey."

Yet Pharaoh's heart became hard and he would not listen to them (Moses and Aaron), just as the Lord had said" (Exod 7:13). There followed a series of plagues, meant to weaken the ruler's resolve. These were of such nature as to challenge the capacity of the Egyptian pantheon to contend with the Sovereign Lord.

Even if select plagues can be explained as resulting from natural causes, they are distinctive in their extent, and as a timely response to Moses' intercession. The final plague, concerning the death of the first-born, appears meant to recall the oppression of God's first-born—his chosen people. Further speculation seems purposeless, not in that we lack for answers, but are at a loss as to what questions are appropriate.

"During the night Pharaoh summoned Moses and Aaron and said, 'Up! Leave my people, you and the Israelites! Go, worship the Lord as you have requested. Take your flocks and herds, as you have said, and go. And also bless me'" (12:31–32). *As you have requested* and *as you have said* suggest his compliance. Then, in conclusion, he invites their benediction.

Meanwhile, the Israelites celebrated the Passover. This was the defining moment in their corporate experience. Deliverance was pending, as was the covenant enactment. Moreover, it had implications not for them alone but for all. Consequently, in Jewish tradition no one is genuinely free as long as any remain in bondage.

When the Pharaoh was told that the Israelites had departed, he and his officials had a change of heart. "What have we done?" they inquired among themselves. "We have let the Israelites go and have lost their services?" (14:5). So they set out in pursuit.

As the Egyptians approached, the people looked up in dismay. "Was it because there were no graves in Egypt that you brought us to the desert to die?" they sarcastically inquired of Moses. "It would have been better for us to serve the Egyptians than to die in the desert!"

"Do not be afraid," Moses replied. "Stand firm and you will see the deliverance the Lord will bring you today. The Lord will fight for you; you need only to be still." Then the Lord instructed his servant to extend his staff over the sea, at which the water was divided—allowing the Israelites to make good their escape. Then, when the Egyptians attempted to pursue, the waters converged on them. Some speculate that this resulted from volcanic activity documented in the region of the Aegean Sea.

In any case, the Israelites celebrated their deliverance from bondage. "I will sing to the Lord, for he is highly exalted," they chorused. "The horse and its rider he has hurled into the sea. The Lord is my strength and my song, he has become my salvation. He is my God, and I will praise him, my father's God, and I will exalt him." As expressed in the memorable lyrics of Thomas Chisholm:

> Great is Thy faithfulness, O God my Father.
> There is no shadow of turning with Thee.
> Thou changest not, Thy compassions they fail not;
> As Thou hast been, Thou forever wilt be.

The Israelites subsequently made their way to Mount Sinai. Its traditional site consists of "a granite ridge, the peaks of which reach about 6,000 feet above sea level. The most conspicuous peak, Jebel Musa (Mountain of Moses), looks out toward a wide plain approximately four miles in length and up to a mile in width."[5] Nestled on the lower slopes of the ridge is the sixth-century Monastery of St. Catherine, which houses a priceless library.

Then Moses went up before the Lord, while the people waited expectantly for his return. "Now if you obey me fully and keep my covenant, then out of all the nations you will be my treasured possession," Moses was instructed to inform the populace. "Although the whole earth is mine, you will be for me a kingdom of priests and a holy nation" (19:5–6). Worthy of note, the priest intercedes not only on his behalf but that of others—in this instance the nations.

Now the covenant took the form of a vassal treaty, whereby the Lord promises to bless the assembly on condition of their faithfulness. In particular, it consists of five segments: the preamble, historical prologue, stipulations, sanctions, and provision for renewal. The *preamble* is succinctly expressed, "Moses proclaimed to the Israelites all that the Lord had commanded him concerning them" (Deut 1:3). Yahweh is thus identified as the heavenly sovereign, who is deserving of reverent obedience.

The *historical prologue*, in turn, recalls the Lord's prior faithfulness. "Benefits allegedly conferred by the Lord upon the vassal were cited with a view to grounding the vassal's allegiance in a sense of gratitude complementary to the sense of fear which the preamble's grandiose identification of the suzerain had been calculated in inspire."[6]

However, it was the *stipulations* that constituted the bulk of the covenant. Some were of a general nature, like the injunction to honor one's parents. "Honor of parents involves respect, obedience, and love. It involves taking care of their physical, social, and spiritual needs. The rab-

---

5. Inch, *Saga of the Spirit*, 13.
6. Kline, *Treaty of the Great King*, 52.

bis reasoned that parental honor should extend beyond life as a treasured memory expressed in attitude and deed."[7] The remaining stipulations dealt with specific instances, such as proper sexual relationships and the protection of property. The rabbis reasoned that this resembled the building of a fence, so that one would not fall prey to temptation. In this regard, an orthodox rabbi inquired of me: "What is wrong with building a fence?" Whereupon, I deferred to him for an answer. "Nothing is wrong with building a fence," he observed, "so long as one does not worship it."

The *sanctions* contrast the results of keeping the covenant and failing to do so. As for the former, "You will blessed in the city and blessed in the country. The fruit of your womb will be blessed, and the crops of your land and the young of your livestock. You will be blessed when you come in and blessed when you go out" (28:3–4, 6). He resembles "a tree planted by streams of water, which yields its fruit in season and whose leaf does not wither" (Psa 1:3).

"Not so the wicked!" the psalmist then exclaims. "They are like chaff that the wind blows away. Therefore the wicked will not stand in the judgment, nor sinners in the assembly of the righteous." In more specific terms, "Cursed is the man who does not uphold the words of this law by carrying them out. Then all the people shall say, 'Amen!'" (Deut 27:26).

Finally, a provision for *covenant renewal* allowed the people to respond to changing circumstances within the covenant framework. Such as when they settled down in the Promised Land, having consummated their wilderness wandering. The covenant thus took on a dynamic character.

As one might expect, the theme of righteousness/justice took on prominence with the covenant. Several examples will serve to illustrate. Initially, "He executes justice for the fatherless and the widow, and loves the stranger, in giving him food and clothing" (Deut 10:18). "God's electing love for Israel has been affirmed to be free of sheer favoritism and so not in conflict with the affirmation that God *shows no impartiality*. The point is now expressed in a converse way. The impartiality of Yahweh is seen in that he not only *loved* Israel but he also *loves* the alien."[8]

Both the Israelites and aliens are thus viewed as works in progress. As expressed by C. S. Lewis, because God loves them, he seeks to make them lovable. Nor is he disposed to settle for less.

---

7. Inch, *Scripture As Story*, 13.
8. Wright, *Deuteronomy*, 149.

"Do not pervert justice or show partiality," the Lord subsequently enjoins. "Do not accept a bribe, for a bribe blinds the eyes of the wise and twists the words of the righteous. Follow justice and justice alone, so that you may live and possess the land the Lord your God is giving you" (16:19–20). In context, they were to appoint judges who would faithfully fulfill their office.

These were to *follow justice and justice alone*, without equivocation. As if oblivious to all else: whether it concerns monetary gain or privilege of some other sort. Not simply on select occasions, but with zealous consistency.

Along a similar line, "Do not deprive the alien or the fatherless of justice, or take the cloak of the widow as a pledge. Remember that you were slaves in Egypt and the Lord your God redeemed you from there. That is why I command you to do this" (24:17). The triad of alien, fatherless, and widow is singled out here and elsewhere as emblematic of those peculiarly vulnerable to abuse (cf. 27:19). In particular, the widow must not be stripped of essential clothing in order to guarantee a loan.

The experience of the Israelites in bondage is cited as an incentive. This is in keeping with the rationale, "Do to others as you would have them do to you" (Luke 6:31). Then not necessarily as they have treated you, but according to righteous resolve.

In addition, Gath, was said to have faithfully executed the justice of Yahweh (cf. 33:21). Thus, genuine justice is portrayed being in accord with the Lord's intent. As such, it may be said to constitute an act of devotion.

Conversely, it must resist all of the pressures to compromise. Some are overt, resulting from external pressures. Some are internal, springing from fear or self-indulgence. All are relentless in their effort to subvert righteous behavior.

As noted earlier, the prophets were charged with furthering the cause of righteousness/justice—as set forth in the covenant. Examples abound. For instance, "In the year that King Uzziah died, I saw the Lord seated on a throne, high and exalted." Above him were seraphs, who were calling to one another: "Holy, holy, holy is the Lord Almighty; the whole earth is full of his glory" (Isa 6:1, 3). Thus began a prophetic ministry that would last for about forty years.

Uzziah's reign had been impressive—even though there was reason for concern. Consequently, Isaiah's vision served to remind him that his confidence must be placed in the sovereign Lord, rather than some transitory official. In proverbial terms, "Unless our hope is in God, it is in vain."

"Stop doing wrong, learn to do right," the oracle enjoins. "Seek justice, encourage the oppressed. Defend the cause of the fatherless, plead the case of the widow " (1:16). "*Justice* comes from the verb 'judge'; the book of Judges shows how judging involves taking decisive action. *Righteousness* denotes what accords with the norm of righteousness embodied in Yahweh."[9] Taken together, they imply faithfully adhering to covenant obligations.

This would entail terminating the present pattern of behavior, and cultivating the ways of the righteous. In this regard, "Though your sins are like scarlet, they shall be as white as snow, though they are red as crimson, they shall be like wool. If you are willing and obedient, you will eat the best from the land." Conversely, if they *resist and rebel*, they will be devoured by the sword. "For the mouth of the Lord has spoken."

"The people walking in darkness have seen a great light; and those living in the land of the shadow of death a light has dawned," the prophet adds (9:2). "For unto us a child is born, to us a son is given, and the government will be on his shoulders. He will reign on David's throne and over his kingdom, establishing and upholding it with justice and righteousness from that time on and forever." While in a more general sense all subsequent rulers were measured by David's righteous example, the text obviously has messianic implications.

We are thereby alerted to the fact *righteousness and justice* will eventually prevail. As for the present, we are to work toward that end. As Jurgen Moltmann aptly observes, being more pulled by the future than driven by the past.

"See, I lay a stone in Zion, a tested stone, a precious cornerstone for a sure foundation; the one who trusts will never be dismayed," the oracle declares. "I will make justice the measuring line and righteousness the plumb line" (28:16–17). God's expertise can certainly be trusted.

In particular, the building is erected along the lines of *righteousness and justice*. Since it serves God's purposes, it will stand the test of time. While all else is destined to fail, eventually.

In these and other ways, we are assured: "For I, the Lord, love justice; I hate robbery and iniquity. In my faithfulness I will reward them

---

9. Goldingay, *Isaiah*, 38.

and make an everlasting covenant with them" (61:8). Since the Lord loves justice, *robbery and iniquity* must be exorcized from the community. The rabbis, in turn, interpreted *robbery* in an extended manner, such as when one diminishes the reputation of another.

They also observed that one must embrace God's gifts if indeed devoted to the Almighty. These consist of life in general, and all wholesome aspects associated with it. Life is good, providing we live it according to the Lord's righteous standards. If not, it amounts to good having gone wrong.

Shifting our focus, the word of the Lord came to Jeremiah during the reign of Josiah, whose ministry extended to the time of the exile. "Before I formed you in the womb, I knew you, before you were born I set you apart; I appointed you as a prophet to the nations," the Lord informed him (Jer 1:5).

"Ah Sovereign Lord," he protested, "I do not know how so speak; I am only a child." In other words, he was notably lacking in qualifications.

No matter! "Now, I have put my words in your mouth. See, today I appoint you over nations and kingdoms to uproot and tear down, to destroy and overthrow, to build and to plant." Both to subvert that which is unacceptable, and to promote all that is good and wholesome.

In greater detail, "Do not trust in deceptive words and say, 'This is the temple of the Lord, the temple of the Lord, the temple of the Lord!' If you really change your ways and your actions and deal with one another justly . . . then I will let you live in this place, in the land I gave your forefathers for ever and ever" (7:4–5, 7). "The false prophets apparently believed that "in an emergency, God would intervene directly to save Zion, His sacred mount. For them, therefore, Temple worship was little better than a charm for averting evil, and they had beguiled the people in to trusting in material buildings, forgetful that God required living persons as His temple."[10]

This, then, is what the Lord requires: "Do what is just and right. Rescue from the hand of the oppressor the one who has been robbed. Do no wrong or violence to the alien, the fatherless or the widow, and do not shed innocent blood in this place" (22:3). Then you will be blessed.

Failing to respond to the prophet's appeal, they can expect the temple to lie in ruins and the people carried off into exile. As C. S. Lewis aptly

---

10. Harrison, *Jeremiah & Lamentations*, 65–66.

acknowledges, only God knows when more time will serve no constructive purpose.

"Do not think that I have come to abolish the Law or the Prophets;" Jesus subsequently declared; "I have not come to abolish them but to fulfill them" (Matt 5:17). However we understand Jesus' comment, he meant to validate the Mosaic appeal to righteousness/justice by way of the school of the prophets.

2

Justice
and the Cardinal Virtues

Raised in a village culture, I primarily associated *virtue* with female chastity. As for males, it was said: "A boy is as good as the girl with whom he hangs out." Probably the nearest male counterpart to female chastity was industry. One was encouraged to secure gainful employment, and care for his family. My father was exemplary in this regard.

The appeal to generosity cut across gender boundaries. Since our back porch opened toward the train station, from time to time a tramp (now designated as *homeless*) would dash from the box-car where he was secreted away to beg for something to eat. Mother would comply, if for no other reason than he was in need. This was only the proverbial tip of the iceberg when it came to her generous disposition.

It would appear that *virtue* is something thought desirable. Homer, for instance, associated it with martial valor. Not surprising, an attempt was made to single out those virtues which were thought to be of most critical importance. These were designated as *cardinal virtues*. According to a commonly accepted appraisal: prudence (wisdom), temperance, fortitude, and justice.

Moreover, the early church fathers added a second category of virtue, designated as *theological* or *special virtues*. As expressed by the apostle Paul, "And now there remains: faith, hope and love. But the greatest of these is love" (1 Cor 13:13). These were thought to be means by which grace enhances the potential of human nature, as created in God's image.

I was assured as a youngster, "A person is known by the company he keeps." With this in mind, we turn our attention to the cardinal virtues—

leaving justice to the last. This will serve to provide a meaningful context in which to consider an admittedly complex virtue.

Prudence. "*Prudence* in its most comprehensive sense is virtually equivalent to *wisdom*. Insofar as it differs, prudence is less religiously explicit. Both alike encourage us to approach life tactfully."[1] In greater detail, "Just as the artisan forges his sword or weaves a rug, so the sage tells us how to live life with finesse. He corrects those of us who blunder along, from one day to the next, saying the wrong thing, doing the wrong thing, wishing we could do better."[2]

As an example of prudent behavior, "Do not plot harm against your neighbor, who lives trustfully near you" (Prov 3:2). Expressed in metaphorical terms, "Let sleeping dogs lie." By way of admonition, "Don't trouble trouble until trouble troubles you."

As another, "Go to the ant, you sluggard, consider its ways and be wise!" (Prov 6:6). In succinct terms, "Been there, and done that." I recall a time as a youth I squatted beside an ant hill, to observe the proceedings more deliberately. Not only was I impressed by the residents' industry, but wondered how they were able to coordinate their endeavor. Did the experience have a profound effect on my life? Only if coupled with other influences too numerous to be detailed.

Prudence does not approach life as a disinterested observer. It rather plunges into the task at hand, as if to live life to its full. In this regard, "Whatever you do, work at it with all your heart, as working for the Lord, not for men, since you know that you will receive an inheritance from the Lord as a reward" (Col 3:23).

Accordingly, my mother would urge from time to time: "Whatever is worth doing is worth doing well." This was a needed reminder for me, since I was disposed to settle for something less than my best—in order to enjoy my leisure.

Conscience plays an ill-defined role in prudent behavior. For instance, while what constitutes modesty differs from one culture to the next, each culture appears to cultivate some perception of modest behavior. This, in turn, brings to mind the observation that the more things change, the more some things appear to remain constant.

As an appeal to conscience, "Dishonest money dwindles away, but he who gathers money little by little makes it grow" (Prov 13:11). This

---

1. Inch, *Why Take the Bible Seriously?*, 50.
2. Inch, *Understanding Bible Prophecy*, 70.

is calculated to encourage one to think it terms of long-range results, rather than settling for something immediate. Especially when the latter involves a lack of credibility.

All things considered, "Where conscience is crippled or stunted, prudence is also impotent and uncertain. A conscience that is sound, alert, forthright is the best guarantee for the correctness of the prudential acts of deliberation and judgment."[3] In this connection, the author of Hebrews confidently affirms: "We are sure that we have a clear conscience and desire to live honorably in every way" (13:18). This leads him to request the intercession of his readers that he might be restored to them without delay.

Prudence also recalls pertinent experience from the past. This involves three concentric circles. Initially, there is the corporate human experience that sets man apart from the rest. Second, there is a cultural component—peculiar to any group of persons. Finally, there is the personal experience—which is unique to each individual. This last aspect involves not only circumstances, but factors in our response. These merge in creative fashion to provide guidance as we encounter the exigencies of life.

By way of illustration, David appears desperate. "My God, my God," he cries out, "why have you forsaken me?" (Psa 22:1). Whereupon, he recalls: "In you our fathers put their trust; they trusted you and you delivered them." This leads him to conclude: "I will declare your name to my brothers; in the congregation I will praise you." In proverbial terms, "All is well that ends well."

Prudence moreover requires a critical appraisal. In this regard, it must ascertain what is of prime concern, by way of distinguishing it from secondary matters. For instance, Jesus criticized the Pharisees: "You give a tenth of your spices—mint, dill and cummin. But you have neglected the more important matters of the law—justice, mercy and faithfulness. You should have practiced the latter, without neglecting the former" (Matt 23:23).

Earlier on, Solomon was called upon to decide a case where each of two women claimed a child as her own. "Bring me a sword," he instructed his attendants (1 Kings 3:24). Whereupon, he commanded them: "Cut the living child in two, and give half to the one and half to the other."

The child's genuine mother exclaimed, "Please, my Lord, give her the living baby! Don't kill him!" Conversely, the imposter spitefully insisted

---

3. Haring, *The Law of Christ*, vol. 1, 506.

that the child not be spared. At this, the magistrate concluded that the woman who would have spared the child's life was the actual parent, and word of his wisdom spread throughout the domain.

Application is likewise a feature of prudence. "Suppose a brother or sister is without clothes and daily food," James speculates. "If one of you says to him, 'Go, I wish you well; keep warm and well fed,' but does nothing about his physical needs, what good is it? In the same way, faith by itself, if it is not accompanied by action, is dead" (2:15–17).

In this and other ways, James insisted that faith without works is ineffective. Herein we are tempted to accent one to the virtual exclusion of the other, whereas James advocates a functioning faith. This, in turn, qualifies as prudent behavior.

Finally, prudence is an advocate of humility. The latter should not be equated with self-effacement, since this is too much taken up with self. Consequently, it is for all practical purposes a negative form of pride.

Moses serves as a prime example. When singled out as God's means for delivering his people from bondage, he protested because of his lack of qualification. This invited the Lord to point out that his enablement would be sufficient. Meanwhile, he had called upon Aaron to compensate for what Moses lacked by way of eloquence.

Temperance. *Temperance* constitutes a second of the cardinal virtues, being joined in this regard with *justice*. In proverbial terms, "not too much or too little." As a certain Greek evangelist would observe periodically, "If we do not eat, we will starve." This was by way of justifying a vigorous appetite.

Conversely, the sage admonishes: "Do not join those who drink too much wine or gorge themselves on meat, for drunkards and gluttons become poor, and drowsiness clothes them in rags" (Prov 23:20–21). Thus, the warning against intoxication and gluttony anticipates the prospect of poverty. Moreover, the allusion to *poverty* recalls as a classic expression of temperance: "give me neither poverty nor riches, but give me only my daily bread. Otherwise, I may have too much and disown you. . . . Or I may become poor and steal, and so dishonor the name of my God" (Prov 30:8-9).

Temperance must be deliberately acquired. Accordingly, it is aptly observed: "We must learn to walk before we can run." This is borne out in the commendation: "Well done, good and faithful servant! You have been faithful with a few things; I will put you in charge of many things" (Matt 25:21).

Accordingly, Clement of Alexandria explores the topic in detail: "But if any necessity arises, commanding the presence of married women, let them be well clothed—without by raiment, within by modesty."[4] Thus modesty serves as a graphic instance of temperance.

Clement subsequently turns his attention to the men present: "It is the part of a temperate man also, if eating and drinking, to take a small portion, and deliberately, not eagerly. Both at the beginning and during the course, and to leave off betimes, and so show his indifference." "Nor are you, in the midst of the repast, to exhibit yourselves hugging your food like wild beasts." "A temperate man, too, must rise before the general company, and retire quietly from the banquet."

We are thus alerted to the fact that temperance introduces a wide range of civil behavior. "Being civil means constantly aware of others and weaving restraint, respect, and consideration into the very fabric of life," P. M. Forni concludes. "But it is not just an attitude of benevolent and thoughtful relating to other individuals; it also entails an active interest in the well-being of our communities and even a concern for the health of the planet on which we live."[5]

As such, civility is exceedingly complex. It conveys the related nuances of respect, consideration, courtesy, kindness, good manners, and the like. Along this line, Paul admonishes: "Be devoted to one another in brotherly love. Honor one another above yourselves. Never be lacking in zeal, but keep your spiritual fervor, serving the Lord" (Rom 12:10-11).

The rabbis reasoned that if one is attentive to little things, he or she is more likely to be faithful with regard to more matters that are significant. Providing, that is, that one does not focus on one to the exclusion of the other. Hypocrisy is a persistent threat to a life of genuine piety.

It goes without saying that civility is likewise good. Good for the person practicing, it, and good for those implicated. As commonly expressed, it amounts to a win/win situation. "Be joyful in hope," Paul further elaborates, "patient in affliction, faithful in payer. Share with God's people who are in need. Practice hospitality."

Conversely, do not give way to retaliation. In greater detail, "Do not repay anyone evil for evil. Be careful to do what is right in the eyes of

---

4. Clement of Alexandria, *The Instructor*, book 2, chapter 7.
5. Forni, *Choosing Civility*, 9.

everybody. If it be possible, as far as it depends on you, live in peace with everyone" (Rom 12:17–18).

"We should, then, take Paul's words at face value: he wants us to commend ourselves before non-Christians by seeking to do those "good things" that non-Christians approve and recognize. (Even so, he) would certainly not want us to have forgotten that the 'good he speaks of throughout these verses is defined in terms of the will of God".[6]

Civility is no less a demanding exercise. One must listen carefully to what others have to say, not necessarily in agreement but out of respect for the other person. Incidentally, some of the best insights come from those seemingly less qualified. This recalls an earnest co-ed who was taking an introductory Bible survey. In this connection, she shared with me the topic of her proposed term paper. I was struck by the originality of her thesis, even though it seemed to have escaped the notice of the academic elite.

Then, too, we ought not presume on the intention of others. "Do not judge, or you will be judged," Jesus cautioned. "For in the same way you judge others, you will be judged, and with the measure you use, it will be measured to you" (Matt 7:1–2).

A related appeal for temperance is evident in the saying, "Expect the best, but prepare for any eventuality." Many who mean well, fail miserably; while many perverse persons are frustrated in their efforts. This invites the satirical observation, "With friends like these, who needs enemies?"

Civility also demands that we disagree without being disagreeable. As a rule, find something than one can commend, while pointing out what we suppose has been overlooked. Preface our comment with the qualification, "It seems to me;" rather than pontificating. Do not lift one's voice as if to demand concurrence.

"A gentle answer turns away wrath, but a harsh word stirs up anger," the sage aptly observes. "The tongue of the wise commends knowledge, but the mouth of the fool gushes folly" (Prov 15:1–2). A genuinely wise person is given to restraint, while his counterpart rambles on and on.

It seems best to terminate the discussion of temperance/civility at this juncture, in keeping with the notion of the former. This, in turn, recognizes that we communicate not only in word but also by deed. Accordingly, one should strive to be consistent.

Fortitude. "It is the role of this virtue (fortitude) to repress the rebellion of the emotions against suffering and death, to discipline and

---

6. Moo, *The Epistle of Romans*, 785.

control all the deep sentiments of fear and terror, if they should attempt to interfere with our generous engagement of the good, even at the cost of life itself."[7] Accordingly, fortitude is that which keeps us pressing on, regardless of opposition, discouragement, or reticence.

As an example, the martyr did not despise life. Quite the reverse; he prized life so highly that he was unwilling to surrender the prospect of eternal life for a modest extension of this life. Then, one that would be plagued with regret.

Patience naturally comes to mind in this connection. Both fortitude and patience imply standing firm, or in parochial terms—*hanging tough*. However, fortitude turns out to be more comprehensive. This leads Thomas Aquinas to conclude that patience constitutes the chief but not exclusive expression of fortitude.

This, in turn, recalls the admonition: "We want each of you to show the same diligence to the very end, in order to make your hope sure. We do not want you to become lazy, but to imitate those who through faith and patience inherit what has been promised" (Heb 6:11–12). In particular, get a good start, maintain a good pace, and finish strong.

The affinity between *generosity* and *fortitude* is more subtle. Generosity requires that one give of him or herself repeatedly. Then, too, whether there is a favorable response or otherwise. This is in keeping with the conviction that righteousness will assuredly triumph, and reap rich dividends.

"Cast your bread upon the waters," the mentor enjoins, "for after many days you will find it again" (Eccles 11:1). The metaphor is derived from the practice of dispatching a ship on a commercial enterprise, which will require considerable time for it to return. One should not despair during the interim.

Justice. Last but not least of the cardinal virtues is *justice*. This, moreover, implies that we should treat others fairly. Initially, because this is God's way of dealing with us (cf. Acts 10:34). In addition, because it is the way we would have others treat us (cf. Luke 6:31). Finally, since it is to our corporate advantage.

Even so, justice turns out to be more complex than we might have imagined. Initially, there is *legal justice*. Persons are to be treated equally before the judiciary. "How long will you defend the unjust and show partiality to the wicked?" God indignantly inquires. "Defend the cause of the

---

7. Haring, *op. cit.*, 525.

weak and fatherless; maintain the rights of the poor and oppressed" (Psa 82:2-3).

"Like cages full of birds, their houses are full of deceit; they have become rich and powerful and have grown fat and sleek," the Almighty complains. "Their evil deeds have no limit; they do not plead the case of the fatherless to win it, they do not defend the rights of the poor" (Jer 5:27-28). They have thereby violated their pledge to maintain justice.

Moreover, there is *distributive justice*. "Distributive justice regulates the measure of privileges, aids, burdens or charge, and obligations of the individual as a member of the community. (One) practices distributive justice as a virtue by accepting uncomplainingly the just distribution of burdens and privileges."[8]

For instance, the task for rebuilding the wall of Jerusalem was parceled out among those available. Consequently, "The Fish Gate was rebuilt by the sons of Hassenaah. They laid its beams and put its door and bolts and bars in place. Meremoth, son of Uriah, the son of Hakkoz, repaired the next section" (Neh 3:3-4).

"The people worked with all their heart" (4:6). They appear not to have complained that their burden was too heavy, or that of others too light. In this regard, they demonstrated confidence in their leaders, and respect for the integrity of their associates.

Not to be overlooked, there is also *commutative justice*. This is meant to regulate the interchange of commodities and services. "Shall I acquit a man with dishonest scales, with a bag of false weights?" God asks the obvious (Micah 6:11). No! Never! It bears repeating: "But let justice roll on like a river, righteousness like a never-failing stream! (Amos 5:22).

On the one hand, the employer is obligated to pay a fair wage. On the other, the employee is responsible to provide a fair return. This accounts for one of my father's favorite sayings, "A fair day's salary for a fair day's work." Furthermore, both should be open to arbitration of their differences.

Finally, there is *retributive justice*. This implies just punishment for wrongdoing. By way of example, "If men who are fighting hit a pregnant woman and she gives birth prematurely but there is no serious injury, the offender must be fined whatever the woman's husband demands and the courts allow" (Exod 21:23). Since there appears to have been no serious injury to the mother or the child, a monetary settlement seems adequate.

8. Ibid., 517.

However, this is conditional of the husband making a claim, and the courts allowing it as legitimate.

"But if there is serious injury, you are to take life for life, eye for eye, tooth for tooth, hand for hand, foot for foot, burn for burn, wound for wound, bruise for bruise." The much expounded *lex talionis*, tit for tat, does not preclude taking into consideration extenuating circumstances. Nor must it be applied in literal manner, but rather according to strict justice.

Conversely, it was intended to preclude excessive punishment. As such, it would discredit Lamech's vindictive boast: "I have killed a man for wounding me, a young man for injuring me. If Cain is avenged seven times, then Lamech seventy-seven times" (Gen 4:23-24).

The Mosaic legislation put heavy emphasis on compensation . For instance, "If a man uncovers a pit or digs one and fails to cover it and an ox or a donkey falls into it, the owner of the pit must pay for the loss; he must pay its owner and the dead animal will be his" (Exod 21:33). If given fair compensation, the owner should not expect to retain the animal as well.

In some instances, the offense was in more general terms. When this was the case, the perpetrator was expected to compensate society in some manner. This might currently translate into rendering community service without remuneration.

Capital punishment was allowed, but not as a rule required. As a result, it was relatively infrequent. This, in turn, brings to mind an incident during Jesus' public ministry. Certain of the scribes and Pharisees brought to Jesus a woman caught in adultery. "In the Law Moses commanded us to stone such women," they observed. "Now what do you say?" (John 8:5). They meant to find cause to accuse him.

Instead of responding, Jesus knelt and started to write on the ground with his finger. When they continued to question him, he straightened up and replied: "If any one of you is without sin, let him be the first to throw a stone at her." Again, he stooped down and continued to write. At this, her accusers began to leave one at a time, beginning with the older ones. Jesus then inquired of her: "Woman, where are they? Has no one condemned you?"

"No one, sir," she said.

"Then neither do I condemn you," Jesus declared. "Go now and leave your life of sin." Thus, justice was served, except from a legalistic point of view. Here we take leave of justice and the cardinal virtues, only to anticipate that they will reemerge.

3

Justice and the Theories

There is perhaps no more urgent appeal today than that for *justice*, nor complaint for its absence. Even so, the meaning is often imprecise. Consequently, this often generates less light than heat.

With this in mind, Karen Lebacqz sets out to discuss six theories concerning justice, although not always identified as such. In this regard, she supposes that justice resembles the proverbial elephant examined by blind-folded explorers. "Each feels a different part—the foot, the ears, the tusks—and consequently each describes the beast differently—gnarled and tough, thin and supple, smooth and hard. The elephant itself—justice—is not encompassed by any of the individual descriptions."[1]

The Utilitarian Theory. Few unqualified utilitarians have survived the criticism of the past century. Conversely, remnants linger in combination with other alternatives—as a testimony to its continuing relevance.

The utilitarian advocates that we should act in such as way as to achieve the greater good. Several considerations come to mind. First, what do we construe as *good*? Jeremy Bentham, for instance, suggests that it consists of what fosters pleasure.

This, in turn, recalls the Epicurean—who judged the value of something in terms of the pleasure or pain associated with it. While this has come to be associated with indulgent behavior, he recognized that momentary pleasure could readily result in enduring pain. Instead, he advocated that persons seek out the more refined aspects of life, as enduring

---

1. Lebacqz, *Six Theories of Justice*, 9.

sources of pleasure. This is associated with a life of moderation, and the cultivation of enduring friendships.

Second, what appears beneficial to one may turn out to be counterproductive for another. This invites the suggestion that we should seek the greater good for the greater number. But who is to determine what constitutes the greater good, or accurately appraise the number favorably implicated? In graphic terms, it seems to advocate that persons play God—a role for which they are strikingly unsuited.

The problem results in part because of the complex features of life. One action solicits an unexpected response from another. Whether for good or evil, our behavior has consequences. In this regard, God is said to "punish the children for the sin of the fathers to the third and fourth generation of those who hate (him), but showing love to a thousand generations of those who love (him) and keep (his) commandments" (Exod 20:5–6). Accordingly, this leads to the observation that if God were to throw dice, they would be loaded.

Third, the quest for justice arises in the context of some set of circumstances. Such as when some are thought not to be getting their due consideration. For instance, when a minority is not proportionately represented.

So it is that justice must contend with various social structures. These, moreover, are approximate means of realizing corporate goals. They can be refined from time to time, and replaced as thought necessary. It is in any case a complex procedure.

Finally, its limitations notwithstanding, classical utilitarianism provides a valuable component to our understanding of justice. In this connection, it provides an explicit method for making difficult decisions; while emphasizing the importance of pleasure as a significant aspect of a theory of justice. This, in turn, makes an important contribution to alternative theories of justice.

The Social Contract Theory. The social contract theory next invites our attention. Imagine that a group of people decides to establish a set of principles by which to determine whether justice is served. If the principles were genuinely fair, one would suppose that they must have the input of those implicated—if not a consensus, then by genuinely representative individuals.

Conversely, no one should be allowed to dominate the intricate process. Nor to take unfair advantage of their superior capabilities or social position. To acknowledge the obvious, "Fair is fair."

As with our constitution, the original document is thought in some manner normative for subsequent behavior. In particular, it can be amended by due process. Then, too, the judiciary not uncommonly employs questionable privilege to modify the intent of the founding fathers. Or so it would seem from the perspective of the more conservative among our number.

Next is the issue of whether we should allow any inequalities in income, wealth, power, and the like. It might initially appear that we should argue for the negative, given a commitment to a fair allotment of resources. However, this proves to be unrealistic. Some will make better use of their opportunities than others, and this will be passed on from one generation to another.

This recalls the contrast between two economic systems; the one pertaining to the Canaanites and the other to the Israelites who in some measure displaced them. As for the former, "Sociological studies indicate that the aristocracy, temple, and government officials, making up about 2 percent of the population of Canaan had control of over 50 percent of the land as patrimony holdings."[2] These holdings were worked by slaves or sharecropping peasants, who returned over half of the produce to their landlords. Villagers, who paid excessive taxes, tilled the remainder of the land.

As for the latter, God was thought to be the ultimate owner of the land. He, in turn, entrusted it not to a privileged class, but tribe by tribe, and family by family. Casting lots in public was an approved means to assuring that the allotment was fair.

Now in a given circumstance, a person might be compelled to sell his allotment either in full or part. However, they were strictly enjoined: "The land shall not be sold in perpetuity, for the land is mine; for you are strangers and sojourners with me" (Lev 25:23). "The term *my* (God's) *tenants* employs the image of extended family or household. The land is God's and a gift to the people. In a sense they are renting it or managing

---

2. Hamlin, *Joshua*, 110.

it on behalf of the divine owner, and the Sabbath and Jubilee customs give explicit practical shape to that view."[3]

Worthy of note, "'Justice as fairness' provides a clear contrast to the utilitarian view. Principles of justice are derived not by assessing the utility of actions but by fair choice in a fair setting. These principles are geared toward the basic structure of society, not toward every act or every level where justice is a concern."[4]

Moreover, the fact that principles are chosen, even under relatively fair circumstances, does not guarantee that they are just. For instance, should one agree to sell a painting for $100 dollars on Monday does not make it a fair price on Wednesday—when it is discovered to be a masterpiece.

This would suggest, at the very least, that there must be procedural considerations to be taken into consideration. These, in addition, are exceedingly difficult to enact, let alone apply with consistency. As with the utilitarian model, the social contract option appears to be a partial truth requiring further definition.

The Entitlement Theory. In brief, Robert Nozick initiates his proposal with a minimal set of fundamental rights: such as protection from injury inflicted by others, freedom of choice and action, and rights to the guarantee of private property. The state is legitimate only insofar as it ensures protection of these rights and compensation for their violation.

In the process, Nozick disallows any notion of distributive justice, limiting justice to the commutative sphere of individual exchanges. By way of illustration, suppose that persons paid Wilt Chamberlain $1 to observe him playing basketball. Each exchange is eminently fair. However, they result in Chamberlain gaining wealth at the shared expense of others. Even so, he ought not to be forced to return his earnings under the guise of justice.

Accordingly, "justice does not consist in promoting the greatest good for the greatest number, nor in protecting the least advantaged. Neither society as a whole nor any individual or group can make claims against the state for the distribution of goods other than that which arises for free exchanges among individuals."[5] While it may be *unfortunate* that some

---

3. Bellinger, Jr., *Leviticus, Numbers*, 150.
4. Lebacqz, *op.cit.*, 40.
5. Ibid., 58.

are wealthier than are others, it is not *unfair*—providing the rules concerning the exchange of goods and services have not been violated.

This gives rise to the notion of a *protective agency*. By implication, this should not exceed the purpose for which it is intended. Nozick anticipates an expansive system of local initiatives, rather than some overarching bureaucracy.

The implications of Nozick's theory are indeed startling. Not only does it suggest that taxes are a form of forced labor, but also provides no *utility floor* for those worst off. In addition, it requires no limits in the disparity between rich and poor, and thus resists a welfare state.

Not surprising, Nozick solicits extensive criticism. In this connection, Bruce Ackerman insists that his notion of basic rights, such as the right to own property, is absolute only in an ideal world, and not in the real world we inhabit. Accordingly, he complains: "Nozick's position is dialogically indefensible in a world deeply scarred by illegitimate domination."[6]

Also, it is said that he fails to understand the implications of commutative justice. Since this requires shared social awareness, and the competence to evaluate the items to be exchanged. This recalls the inability of American students to cope with the expertise of Arab merchants in Jerusalem. Conversely, the latter more than met their match when confronted with African students, who had refined their talents for bargaining.

It appears, then, that there are serious problems with the entitlement theory, not unlike those that preceded it. Nozick has himself pointed out some of the deficiencies in his model, such as a clearer analysis of what constitutes private property, and the complex nature of harmful activity. In addition, his critics point to underlying issues: as an inadequate notion of human nature, and the application of simple norms to a complex capitalistic society.

Conversely, he makes a valiant effort to point out the historical roots to justice, and accent the critical importance of commutative justice—whether in this instance or that of some alternative model. Then, finally, he is sensitive to the tension between liberty and equality. One may opt to minimize one at the expense of the other.

---

6. Ackerman, *Social Justice in the Liberal State*, 186.

A Catholic Response. Given the provocative nature of the public debate, one would expect a response from the Catholic prelates. Consequently, The National Conference of Catholic Bishops issued a second draft of a pastoral letter on Catholic social teaching and the U. S. economy in 1985. It represented a Catholic approach to social and distributive justice.

Allowing for recent developments with Vatican II and related events, the Catholic tradition on social teachings is rooted in three basic affirmations: "(1) the inviolable dignity of the human person, (2) the essentially social nature of human beings, and (3) the belief that the abundance of nature and of social living is given for all people."[7]

As for *the dignity of the human person*, individuals are not to be manipulated—as if they were simply inanimate objects. Accordingly, their opinions are to be respected. Their feelings are also a matter of concern. A legitimate effort must likewise be made to reconcile divergent perspectives.

As for *the essentially social nature of human beings*, persons are not isolated entities, but associated with others. This is notably obvious both with the immediate and extended family. It also applies to a broad range of primary and secondary relationships. Some of these result from our social structure, while others are of voluntary nature.

Finally, as for *the belief that the abundance of nature and of social living is given for all people*, life is meant to be shared. This precludes the more affluent nations from taking advantage of those less fortunate. Moreover, "From the Patristic period to the present, the Church has affirmed that misuse of the world's resources or appropriation of them by a minority of the world's population betrays the gift of creation since 'whatever belongs to God belongs to all.'"[8]

Even so, such programs as call for participation are to be preferred to those that involve only distribution. As expressed in the memorable words of John F. Kennedy: "Ask not what the country can do for you, but what you can do for your country." Desist from being part of the problem, and become part of its resolution.

The fundamental issue contained in the bishop's letter is whether we understand justice to be grounded in a self-interested social contract or with reference to a compassionate deity. If the former, we are hard pressed

---

7. Lebacqz, *op. cit.*, 91.
8. *Bishops Letter*, 40.

to persuade persons that altruistic behavior is necessarily in their best interests. If the former, there remains the problem of how to apply the religious ideal to given situations.

I recall an interchange some years ago with the erudite philosopher Arthur Holmes. In response to my inquiry as to what he had recently written, he indicated that it concerned ethics. When I pressed him concerning his thesis, he replied: "Without God, there isn't any." One would get the impression that the bishops would be in thorough agreement.

Nevertheless, the resulting dilemma is not readily resolved. In particular, how is one to reconcile revelation with reason? Augustine perhaps said it best, "All truth is God's truth." However, not all that passes as true is in fact true. As a result, we would expect both continuity and change with the passing of time. As I have observed on other occasions, the more some things change, the more others appear constant. This lends itself to the bishop's confidence in natural theology, with its emphasis on the common good, reason, and consensus.

A Protestant Alternative. The prominent American theologian Reinhold Niebuhr provides an insightful alternative to the bishops' agenda. Being critical of capitalism, he tentatively considered aspects of Marxism in the course of his studies. However, he eventually complained that the latter alternative turned out to be worse than the disease that it was meant to cure.

He is especially noted for his accent on *realism*, as opposed to abstract speculation. In a world permeated by sin, no single principle or approach will suffice to remedy the situation. As an example, Nozick's preference for the free exchange of the market system ignores the fact that humans will persist in seeking an unfair advantage in exchange. Accordingly, the resulting division of goods will inevitably be unjust.

Instead, justice must be characterized first by achieving a balance of power. This serves as a means of protecting the more vulnerable members of society. In particular, it does not focus on meeting the needs of the marginal, but empowering them to meet their own needs.

This is not the end of the matter, since every solution falls short of its intent. In more detail, "Every relative justice is a relative injustice as well. One can never rest satisfied that justice has been done simply because 'the greatest good' has been done or the disadvantaged are better off than they were before, or exchanges are fair, or living wages are granted."[9] Not in the real world, which is the only world that matters.

In terms of the military metaphor, the quest for justice resembles an attempt to attain high ground. In other words, to secure a place of advantage—from which some future success may be anticipated. Consequently, there are no simple solutions or short cuts in the search for justice.

The critics of Niebuhr are legion, as there are those who defend him. The most inclusive charge is that his posturing allows for no theory by which to appraise justice. In this connection, Emil Brunner pointedly concluded that he had never worked out a clear concept of justice—which could evaluate matters. In metaphorical terms, "It is hard to hit a target, if you do not have one."

By way of rebuttal, Niebuhr associates justice with love. In a manner of speaking, justice is love in action. As such, it has no independent identity. In this regard, he argues that while love can exceed justice, it can never abrogate it.

Nonetheless, the critics protest that his approach not only leads to ambiguity, but also fosters conflict. For instance, if justice assumes the legitimacy of self-interest and love advocates sacrifice, these appear in opposition to one another. Only if we think of love in absolute terms, rather than appreciating the fact that it is expressed in a less than ideal setting.

It would seem that *hard love* factors justice into the equation. As C. S. Lewis observes, "Since God loves us, he seeks to make us lovable." This would seem at least compatible with Niebuhr's line of reasoning.

Still, it would prove helpful if he were to establish some procedural rules for ascertaining justice. In other words, what does his appeal to justice amount to in practical terms? Short of this, it would seem to fall prey to situation ethics.

Niebuhr's mistrust of human ideology and initiatives raises doubt concerning the credibility of social ethics. Along with this, the quest for justice seems suspect. Conversely, this allows for revelation as an instrumental means of guiding our endeavors. Not to the exclusion of other considerations, but as a divine catalyst in the human enterprise. If so, we are much the better for Niebuhr's sage counsel.

A Liberation Challenge. Liberation theology views justice from the perspective of the oppressed. It supposes that God especially favors them

---

9. Lebacqz, *op. cit.*, 91.

as they strive for justice. Initially, it should be noted that *the poor* in biblical perspective are such as turn to God in their distress. There is no virtue in being poverty stricken as such.

Now it seems profitable to approach the topic in an indirect fashion, with reference to what is referred to as *the gospel of wealth*. In particular, Russell Conwell's often delivered sermon *Acres of Diamonds*—which was by way of encouraging persons to make the most of their opportunities.

At one point, he allows for the criticism that he enjoins people to gain wealth, instead of admonishing them to embrace the gospel. Whereupon, he replied: "To make money honestly is preaching the gospel." When pressed further, he offered the opinion that 98 of 100 percent of affluent men in America were honest. Accordingly, he supposed that wealth was a general indication of piety.

The contrast between these two perspectives is obvious: one insists that God intervenes on behalf of the oppressed, while the other is of the opinion that he acknowledges the stewardship of the affluent. However, both alike suggest that the Almighty is more amenable to one class than to another.

Walter Brueggemann appears to provide a more compelling case, with his focus on shalom for *haves* and *have-nots*. As for the former, he cites as representative: "Judah and Israel were as many as the sand by the sea; they ate and drank and were happy" (1 Kgs 4:20). As for the latter, "He saved them from the hand of their enemies all the days of the judge; for the Lord was moved to pity by their groaning because of those who afflicted and oppressed them" (Judg 2:18).

"My point here is a simple but nonetheless important one," Brueggeman insists. "People who are well-off have very different perceptions of life and a very different theological agenda from those who must worry about survival. Both are in the Bible, and while (we have taken the) theology of survival seriously, (we have been less alert to) the Bibles' theology of management and celebration."[10]

This, in turn, recalls a pertinent text: "From everyone who has been given much, much will be demanded; and from the one who has been entrusted with much, much more will be asked" (Luke 12:48). Consequently, while all are required to give an accounting, some have more to work with

---

10. Brueggemann, *Living Toward a Vision*, 30.

than do others. Moreover, this extends beyond monetary matters to embrace any sort of privilege—as with general health and training.

As a result, this third option tends to eliminate the temptation to demonize others, while assuming God's blessing. In any case, one would gather that God's grace is sufficient to meet any challenge. In short, the pursuit of justice seems to revolve around the opportunity to maximize one's potential. In this regard, it affirms Niebuhr's appeal for realism.

As for the liberation challenge, God's intervention in history is decidedly not limited to his deliverance of the poor and oppressed. He is the sovereign Lord of all, requiring righteous resolve. This ideally embraces both the haves and have-nots in an ongoing struggle to acquire justice.

All things considered, we are left to reflect on the elephant metaphor. Each perceives justice from a limited perspective. This fragmented purview cautions humility, and earnest dialogue. Otherwise, our well-meaning efforts can prove our undoing.

4

Justice and Faith

The previous chapter has subtly turned our attention to the theological/spiritual virtues mentioned earlier. In particular, faith, hope, and love. These were highlighted in the context of redemptive history, so that righteousness/justice appears in connection with our relationship to God and one another.

"Now faith is being sure of what we hope for and certain of what we do not see" (Heb 11:1). There were in former times "many men and women who had nothing but the promises of God to rest upon, without any visible evidence that these promises would ever be fulfilled; yet so much did these promises mean to them that they regulated the whole course of their lives in their light."[1]

"Blessed are they who maintain justice, who constantly do what is right," the psalmist acknowledges (106:3). Since it may not appear so at any given moment, one has only *the promises of God* on which to rely. These provide not simply assurance, but enablement. In metaphorical terms, one *walks* by faith.

"This is what the ancients were commended for," the text of Hebrews continues. Not for their exploits alone, but their availability to God's leading. Accordingly, the distinction between *faith* and *trust* is subtle, if intended. Otherwise, the latter appears more subjective.

"By faith Abraham, when called to go to a place he would later receive as his inheritance, obeyed and went, even though he did not know

---

1. Bruce, *The Epistle of Hebrews*, 276.

where he was going." His faith was evident in his obedience. Nothing is said of his inclination, although one would assume that he had grave misgivings. His departure would leave behind familiar circumstances and the support of an extended family.

Then, too, the alternative was not inviting. He had little understanding of what awaited him. Nor could he predict how he would react given the variables.

Even so, we are told that God had promised this land to him as an inheritance. It remained for him to exercise faith. Then, in this manner, to encourage others to respond similarly. Assured, in the refrain of the gospel song: "The God on the mountain is the God in the valley"—one and the same in good times and bad.

The pursuit of justice follows an analogous route. We are called upon to leave a situation where we feel relatively confident, to explore new possibilities. Some will misunderstand our motives. It may appear that we are swimming against the current. What are we to do? Press on, in faith believing that God's ways are best.

"By faith he made his home in the promised land like a stranger in a foreign country, he lived in tents, as did Isaac and Jacob, who were heirs with him of the same promise." As for those who emulate the patriarch, "They pass their days on earth, but are citizens of heaven. They obey the prescribed laws, and at the same time, they surpass the laws by their lives. They love all men, and are persecuted by all."[2]

More to the point, "Wherefore they do not commit adultery nor fornication, nor bear false witness, nor embezzle what is held in pledge, nor covet what is not theirs. They honor father and mother, and show kindness to those near to them; and whenever they are judges, they judge uprightly."[3] Accordingly, they promote justice.

"For he was looking forward to the city with foundations, whose architect and builder was God." This is to say, a city with firm foundations. One that can withstand the assault of the enemy. One also that is immune from the ravages of time. Here faith and hope converge, along with loving devotion.

"By faith Abraham, even though he was past age—and Sarah herself was barren—was enabled to become a father because he considered

---

2. *Letter to Diognetus*, iv.
3. *The Apology if Aristide*, xv.

him faithful who had made the promise." Subsequently, his descendants would become "as numerous as the stars in the sky and as countless as the sand on the seashore." *The stars in the sky* and *sand on the seashore* are idiomatic allusions to a great number.

Time thus factors into the faith/justice equation. In proverbial terms, "Rome was not built in a day." In greater detail, "All these people were still living by faith when they died. They did not receive the things promised; they only saw them and welcomed them from a distance, and they admitted that they were aliens and strangers on earth." Accordingly, the rabbis rightly concluded that the times and seasons were in the inscrutable hands of the Almighty.

As a result, life resembles an earnest of the future. This, in turn, requires that we make do with what we have available. In terms of justice, we must content ourselves with approximations. While not ideal, they are nonetheless constructive.

An especially pertinent incident in the patriarch's life next solicits our consideration. "The Lord appeared to Abraham near the great tree of Mamre while he was sitting at the entrance of his tent in the heat of the day" (Gen 18:1). As for commentary, "The goatskin tents of pastoral nomadic people were designed to hold in heat at night with the flaps down and to allow a breeze to pass through during the day, when the flaps were up."[4] Sitting at the entrance during the heat of the day would provide shade while allowing persons to enjoy the breeze and guard the contents of the enclosure.

When Abraham looked up, he saw three men standing by. It was customary to stand within sight of the encampment, awaiting an invitation. If for some reason the prospective host were indisposed, he would offer a polite excuse. In one instance that comes to mind, the host indicated that one of his sheep was seriously ill.

In any case, hospitality was for all practical purposes considered a sacred obligation. It provided a critical service, by way of sustenance and security. It was also thought to be a welcomed opportunity, not to be undertaken in a begrudging manner. Accordingly, the patriarch hurried from the entrance to his tent, and bowed low to the ground—in anticipation of rendering hospitality.

---

4. Walton and Matthews, *Genesis-Deuternomy*, 44.

"If I have found favor in your eyes, my lord, do not pass your servant by," he employed. "Let a little water be brought, and then you may all wash your feet and rest under this tree. Let me get you something to eat, so you can be refreshed and then go on your way."

"Very well," they replied, "do as you say." Whereupon, he had food prepared for them. While they ate, he stood near them under the tree. "Where is your wife Sarah?" they inquired of him.

"There, in the tent," he observed. This was also according to custom, since the wife was to see to the preparation of food, while her husband visited with the guests. On one occasion, I recall that the wife was greatly interested in the subject we were discussing, and lingered within hearing distance. At one point, she discreetly engaged in the discussion—offering her insights.

"I will surely return to you about this time next year," the Lord informed Abraham, and Sarah your wife will have a son." Now Sarah was listening at the entrance of the enclosure, and laughed to herself at the thought of bearing a child at her advanced stage in life. "Why did Sarah laugh?" the Lord protested. "Is anything too hard for the Lord?" Then he assured the patriarch that this would indeed come to pass.

Is anything too hard for the Lord? This became a recurring theme in the biblical text. God is not plagued by human restrictions. Conversely, he *does not* violate his righteous resolve—whether in terms of justice or some other instance. Nor does he act in such a way as to negate human response to his gracious initiatives. In either instance it would involve a contradiction in terms.

As a matter of record, he often employs modest means to accomplish great things. This, in turn, recalls a time when my wife and I visited one of my Nigerian students—at the invitation of her father. I was surprised upon entering their church sanctuary to view the portrait of an expatriate displayed behind the pulpit. Upon inquiring, I was told that she was responsible for bringing the gospel to that region.

It seems that the British authorities refused her permission to enter the district, for fear that it would offend the Muslim constituency. However, she reasoned that there was a higher authority who over-ruled this prohibition. She then endured a demanding trek to a remote area. As a result, this became a focus of Christian outreach and educational activity. We are thus enjoined to not only expect great things for God, but to undertake great things in his name.

When the visitors got up to leave, they looked down toward Sodom. Abraham walked with them briefly, as a token expression of his goodwill. Whereupon, the Lord reflected: "Shall I hide from Abraham what I am about to do?" Especially seeing that he "will surely become a great and powerful nation, and all nations will be blessed through him." Since he would become the means of disclosing God's righteous ways to subsequent generations.

Then the Lord said to him, "The outcry against Sodom and Gomorrah is so great and their sin so grievous that I will go down and see if what they have done is as bad as the outcry that has reached me." If confirmed, the implication is that he would chastise them for their wickedness.

When the strangers had turned away toward Sodom, the patriarch remained standing before the Lord. "Will you sweep away the righteous with the wicked?" Abraham speculated. "What if there are fifty righteous people in the city? Will you really sweep it away and not spare the place for the sake of the fifty righteous people in it? Far be it from you to do such a thing—to kill the righteous with the wicked, treating the righteous and the wicked alike."

"Far be it from you!" he exclaimed. "Will not the judge of the earth do right?" "The premise of this question is that those who live righteously generate moral value that acts as a preservative of a corrupt society threatened by judgment. . . . His premise was that it would be uncharacteristic of God's nature *to kill the righteous with the wicked*."[5]

Whereupon, the Lord assured him: "If I find fifty righteous people in the city of Sodom I will spare the whole place for their sake." We would thus conclude that justice is refined to take into consideration the complex nature of society, and not simply as the result of a simple correlation.

"Now that I have been so bold as to speak to the Lord, though I am nothing but dust and ashes," the patriarch allows, "what if the number of the righteous is five less than fifty? Will you destroy the whole city because of five people?" This was in keeping with the custom of bargaining, prevalent in the market place.

This, moreover, recalls a time when three students accompanied me to the shop of an Arab dealer in antiquities. While sipping tea, the dealer and I engaged in an attempt to reach a mutually satisfactory agreement. This went on for about a half hour, before we concluded our negotiations.

---

5. Hartley, *op. cit.*, 182.

As we were making our way back to school, the students expressed their amazement over what had transpired—since it was quite alien to their culture.

"If I find forty-five there," the Lord allowed, "I will not destroy it." It appeared as a gracious concession.

"What if only forty are found there?" the patriarch continued.

"For the sake of forty," the Lord again acquiesced, "I will not do it."

"May the Lord not be angry," Abraham pled. "What if only thirty can be found there?" Incidentally, the detailed dialogue is likely for the purpose of oral transmission, which played a prominent role in a semi-literate society.

"I will not do it if I find thirty there," the Sovereign assured him.

As if throwing caution to the wind, the patriarch observed: "Now that I have been so bold as to speak to the Lord, what if only twenty can be found there?"

"For the sake of twenty, I will not destroy it," the Lord resolutely responded.

"May the Lord not be angry," Abraham again petitioned, "but let me speak just once more. What if only ten can be found there?" Surely he must have thought there were at least ten righteous persons residing in this cesspool of iniquity.

Whereupon, he answered: "For the sake of ten, I will not destroy it." The two then went their separate ways. As a matter of record, Sodom was laid waste—as a testimony to its pervasive degradation. This, in turn, recalls the wisdom saying: "Justice is and justice does."

The author of Hebrews next refers to the *akeda* (*binding* of Isaac). The Jewish tradition dwells on this episode more than any other recorded in sacred writ. Not only is Abraham considered as exemplary of those who walk by faith, but also concerning virtually every conceivable virtue—justice being no exception.

"By faith Abraham, when God tested him, offered Isaac as a sacrifice" (Heb 11:17). In greater detail, "He who had received the promises was about to sacrifice his one and only son, even though God has said to him, 'It is through Isaac that your offspring will be reckoned.' Abraham reasoned that God could raise the dead, and figuratively speaking, he did receive Isaac back from the dead."

In still greater detail, God set out to test the righteous resolve of the patriarch. "Abraham!" he summoned him (Gen 22:1).

"Here I am," the patriarch compliantly answered. In a manner of speaking, he was at God's service.

Then God said, "Take your son, your only son, Isaac, whom you love, and go to the region of Moriah. Sacrifice him there as a burnt offering on one of the mountains I will tell you about." The three-fold injunction was meant to insure that the task would be carried out.

"Texts from Phoenician and Punic colonies, like Carthage in North Africa, describe the ritual of child sacrifice as a means of insuring continued fertility. The biblical prophets and the laws in Deuteronomy and Leviticus expressly forbid this practice, but that also implies that it continued to occur."[6] It may be that at this juncture the patriarch had not clearly distinguished between the contrasting perspectives. Then, too, according to the text of Hebrews, Abraham thought that Isaac would survive the ordeal.

Early the next morning the patriarch set about to make the journey. He took with him two of his servants, along with his son Isaac. On the third day, he looked up, and saw the appointed place in the distance. "Stay here with the donkey while I and the boy go over there," he said to the servants. "We will worship and then we will come back to you."

Abraham then took the wood for the burnt offering, and delivered it to his son, while he carried the fire and knife. As the two walked on together, Isaac observed: "The fire and wood are here, but where is the lamb for the burnt offering?"

"God himself will provide the lamb for the burnt offering, my son," his father replied. Whereupon, the two continued on together. This was calculated to express the close bond between them.

When they reached the designated place, the patriarch built an altar and arranged the wood on it. Then he bound his son, and laid him on top of the pile of wood. After that, he reached out his hand to slay Isaac. This incited the angel of the Lord to protest: "Do not lay a hand on the boy. Do not do anything to him. Now I know that you fear God, because you have not withheld from me your son, your only son."

Whereupon, Abraham looked up and saw a ram caught by its horns in a thicket. He went over, took the ram, and sacrificed it, instead of his son. Consequently, he identified the place *The Lord Will Provide*. This,

---

6. Walton and Matthews, *op. cit.*, 49.

moreover, assumed the form of a proverb: "On the mountain of the Lord it will be provided."

Then the angel of the Lord called out a second time: "I swear by myself, declares the Lord, that because you have done this and have not withheld your son, your only son, I will surely bless you and make your descendants as numerous as the stars in the sky and as the sand on the seashore." They will prevail against their enemies, and be a blessing to all nations.

Initially, this "clearly and unequivocally teaches that Yahweh, the only God, never accepts human sacrifice. If God did not accept the sacrifice of Isaac, the first child of promise, surely no other sacrifice of a child would be acceptable to him."[7] If for no other reason, because it would be a violation of justice.

Then, as noted earlier, the Jews drew consolation from this passage to face indignities and oppression they were called upon to endure. "Why the Jews?' Dennis Prager and Joseph Telushkin rhetorically inquire. "Throughout their history Jews have regarded Jew-hatred as an inevitable consequence of their Jewishness." In greater detail, four particulars: their distinctiveness as a chosen people, their attempt to alter the world for the better, their privileged mission, and the quality of life thus enhanced.[8]

Finally, this episode is inexorably linked to the gift of God's one and only Son. "God displayed justice in providing a substitute for Isaac. In the case of his obedient Son Jesus, God proved committed to justice by raising him from the dead. Jesus empowered the promises to Abraham to extend to all the families of the earth."[9] Thus justice is served in both instances, albeit by different means. Accordingly, the sage enjoins: "Trust in the Lord with all your heart and lean not on your own understanding. In all your ways acknowledge him, and he will make your paths straight" (Prov 3:5–6).

---

7. Hartley, *op.cit.*, 212.
8. Prager and Telushkin, *Why the Jews?*, 22–23.
9. Hartley, *op. cit.*, 213.

5

Justice and Hope

While *faith* and *hope* are closely associated, the latter shifts the focus from the present to the future. This embraces the prospect of divine judgment and its ensuing results. Accordingly, it highlights God's righteous justice.

Initially, we will consider two of Jesus' parables in reverse order, before turning to a classic apocalyptic vision. "When the Son of Man comes in his glory, and all the angels with him, he will sit on his throne in heavenly glory," Jesus solemnly declared. "All the nations will be gathered before him, and he will separate the people one from another as a shepherd separates the sheep from the goats. He will put the sheep on his right and the goats on his left" (Matt 25:31–33). Strictly speaking, the scene is not that of a trial, but the passing of a sentence already in hand.

"Although sheep and goats grazed together, it is said that Palestinian shepherds normally separated sheep and goats at night because goats need to be warm at night while sheep prefer open air."[1] This, in turn, would suggest that it was a common practice associated with shepherding.

In terms of their respective temperament, the sheep were more amenable. They seem content under the watchful eye of their shepherd. Although they often wander off, and may fall prey to some wild beast.

The goat appears more spirited, and prone to creating problems. "Goats, then, are most often associated in Scripture with sin in one way or another. In the sacrificial system goats carried sin, and in Jesus' parable,

---

1. Keener, *New Testament*, 118.

they are the ones whose sin has not been forgiven."² Even to the present, we refer to the athlete whose lapse resulted in a loss as *the goat*.

"You have made known to me the path of life, you will fill me with joy in your presence, with eternal pleasures at your right hand," the psalmist enthusiastically anticipated (16:11). Consequently, the people were to recite the blessings associated with the covenant from Mount Gerizim—oriented to the right as one faces to the east, and the curses from Mount Ebal—thus on the left hand (cf. Deut 11:29–30).

"Come, you who are blessed by my Father; take your inheritance, the kingdom prepared for you since the creation of the world," the magistrate invites the faithful. "For I was hungry and you gave me something to eat, I was thirsty and you gave me something to drink, I was a stranger and you invited me in. I needed clothes and you clothed me, I was sick and you looked after me, I was in prison and you came to visit me."

These appear perplexed, and ask for a clarification. They receive by way of response: "I tell you the truth, whatever you did for one of the least of these brothers of mine, you did for me." Even if meant as a reference to Jesus' followers, it would appear to have a broader application.

Turning to those on his left, he enjoins them: "Depart from me, you who are cursed, into the eternal fire prepared for the devil and his angels." After which, he details their unavailability to those who were hungry, thirsty, strangers, without adequate clothing, sick, and in prison.

"Lord," they inquire, "when did we see you hungry or thirsty or a stranger or needing clothes or sick or in prison, and did not help you?" They, too, appear astonished at his pronouncement.

He responded, "I tell you the truth; whatever you did not do for one of the least of these, you did not do for me." Then they will be banished to eternal punishment, while the righteous accorded everlasting life. As for the latter, the emphasis is on the superlative quality of life—not to the exclusion of its duration. We are thus lead to conclude that quality has enduring value.

Although the sacred text clearly teaches that deeds of kindness in themselves do not warrant salvation, it also insists that genuine faith must express itself in concern for others. In other words, it promotes a faith that generates good works.

---

2. Ryken, Wilhoit, and Longman III (eds.), *Dictionary of Biblical Imagery*, 332.

In Jewish tradition, a *mitzvah* is usually translated as *commandment*, although it has come to be expressed as *good deed*. In any case, it is something God stipulates—whether expressly or by implication. It is customary to acknowledge 613 *mitzvot*: 365 negative and 248 positive. These embrace our relationship with the Almighty, and one another. Accordingly, the first positive *mitzvah* pertains to belief in God, while the negative counterpart prohibits belief in any other alleged deity. In this connection, idolatry is said to be the ultimate source for sinful behavior.

In more general terms, the *mitzvot* are designed to point out "our obligation to 'be holy' as God is holy. Thus, our intentions are not to be dismissed completely from a consideration of performing *mitzvot*. But it is a keystone of Jewish belief that one can only come to understand the *mitzvot* by doing them, by imitating God."[3]

"Not everyone who says to me, 'Lord, Lord,' will enter the kingdom of God," Jesus accordingly cautioned, "but only he who does the will of my Father who is in heaven" (Matt 7:21). On the day of judgment false prophets will protest that they have prophesied, drove out demons, and worked miracles—only to be declared *evil-doers*, quite out of touch with the Savior.

"You know that those who are regarded as rulers of the Gentiles lord it over them, and their high officials exercise authority over them," Jesus allowed. "Not so with you. Instead, whoever wants to become great among you must be your servant, and whoever wants to be first must be slave of all. For even the Son of Man did not come to be served, but to serve, and to give his life a ransom for many" (Mark 19:42–45). So we would gather from his insistence that we serve *the least of these*.

As a relevant aside, we consider a familiar passage from the Psalter. "The Lord is my shepherd, I shall not want," the psalmist declares (23:1). His grace is not simply sufficient but abundant. The theme is borne out throughout the text, so that *I shall not want* could readily be employed as a refrain.

"He makes me to lie down in green pastures, he leads me beside quiet waters, he restores my soul." As relates to times of refreshing, it is calculated to restore one's energy and resolve. Thereby to persist in the face of obstacles and discouragement. Then as a reminder that it is always too soon to terminate our service.

---

3. Robinson, *Essential Judaism*, 223.

"He guides me in paths of righteousness for his name's sake." This recalls the rocky paths crisscrossing the Judean hill country. One can readily lose his or her way without someone who is familiar with the terrain.

"Even though I walk through the valley of the shadow of death, I will fear no evil, but you are with me, your rod and your staff, they comfort me." This recalls the deep ravines. These create a sense of foreboding. However, *even* here the Lord's presence is reassuring.

"You prepare a table before me in the presence of my enemies. You anoint my head with oil; my cup overflows." This is by way of hospitality. Moreover, it brings to mind an occasion when my wife and I were invited to the home of an Arab merchant residing in Bethlehem. While appreciative, I was concerned that our vehicle might be torched. However, our host assured us that the greatest care would be taken that such would not happen. The psalmist is no less assured that the Lord would provide security.

Whereupon, the psalmist concludes: "Surely goodness and love will follow me all the days of my life, and I will dwell in the house of the Lord forever." *Goodness and love* resemble two faithful guard dogs, accompanying the flock on its journey. The shepherd walks on ahead, the flock following, and the dogs circling back and forth. This is in anticipation of unmitigated blessings. Such is the provocative imagery of hope.

"Again, it (the consummation) will be like a man going on a journey, who called his servants and entrusted his property to them" (Matt 25:14). He gave to one five talents, to another two, and to a third one talent—"each according to his ability." Thus, it was assumed that those to whom more was given, the more would be required. Then, too, that the Lord would not require more of one than appropriate.

Now the one with five talents gained five more, and the one with two gained an additional two. "But the man who had received the one talent went off, dug a hole in the ground and hid his master's money."

After a long time, the master returned and demanded an accounting of his servants' stewardship. "Well done, good and faithful steward!" he commended the servant who had ten talents to show for his conscientiousness. "You have been faithful with a few things; I will put you in charge of many things. Come and share your master's happiness!" In like manner he congratulated the servant who presented him with four talents.

Conversely, the man with a single talent observed: "I knew that you are a hard man, harvesting where you have not sown and gathering where you have not scattered seed. So I was afraid and hid your talent in the ground. See, here is what belongs to you." "The slave rationalizes his failure to do anything with the talent entrusted to him by blaming his master! His master is a harsh and rapacious businessman, who extracts far more from a business transaction than is his proper due."[4]

"Take the talent from him and give it to the one who has the ten talents," his master countered. "For everyone who has will be given more, and he will have an abundance. Whoever does not have, even what he has will be taken from him. And throw that worthless servant outside, into the darkness, where there will be weeping and gnashing of teeth." This, in turn, recalls Jesus' use of the Valley of Hinnom as a portrait of hell. Here was cast that which no longer served the purpose for which it was made, such as pieces of broken pottery. As for the *weeping and gnashing of teeth*, this would seem to couple remorse with anger. C. S. Lewis seems to confirm this thesis when attributing hell to a loving God for those who will accept nothing better. Then, too, only God knows when more time will serve no constructive purpose.

We now turn our attention from select parables to an impressive apocalyptic vision. Even a casual reading of the text of Revelation would suggest that it was composed at a time of impending persecution. In this regard, while an oppressive power looms on the horizon, the churches addressed by John are able to pursue their ministry. This was most likely during the reign of Domitian (AD 81–96).

The ascription reads, "The revelation of Jesus Christ, which God gave him to show his servants what must soon take place" (Rev 1:1). This serves a dual purpose. "First, it situates the composition within a particular literary and theological tradition: apocalypticism. Within this tradition, the idea of revelation refers to a process whereby God makes known through visions the final days of salvation history."[5]

Second, it validates the author's authority. This is in terms of the *shaliach* tradition, where the one sent is as the one who commissions him. In particular, John is to be received as Jesus' emissary.

"Blessed is the one who reads the words of this prophecy, and blessed are those who hear it and take to heart what is written in it, because the

---

4. Hare, *Matthew*, 287.
5. Wall, *Revelation*, 51.

time is at hand." Such as would enhance a vibrant hope, in keeping with divine justice.

Expanding on this thesis, John addresses seven Asian churches (cf. chapters. 2–3). "The entire sequence is a literary composition designed to impress upon the church universal the necessity of patient endurance in the period of impending persecution. In the final conflict between Christ and Caesar, believers will need to hold fast to their confession of faith and stand ready for whatever sacrifice may be required."[6]

"After this I looked, and there before me was a door standing open in heaven. And the voice I first heard speaking to me like a trumpet said, 'Come up here, and I will show you what must take place after this'" (4:1). This constitutes a clear transition into the heavenly realm. "And it is this chapter of wonderful doxologies that introduces the seven congregations to Revelation's essential theological conviction: God is the eternal creator in whom all things have their meaning and find their importance."[7]

In greater detail, "At once I was in the Spirit, and there before me was a throne in heaven with someone sitting on it. And the one who sat there had the appearance of jasper and carnelian. A rainbow, resembling an emerald, encircled the throne. Surrounding the throne were twenty-four other thrones, and seated on them were twenty-four elders. They were dressed in white, and had crowns of gold on their heads."

A *throne* appears more than forty times in the text of Revelation. As such, it conveys the notion of divine sovereignty. The one sitting on the throne is revealed in awesome splendor. The twenty-four elders were variously accounted for, ranging from angelic attendants to human counterparts.

The graphic description continues. "From the throne came flashes of lightning, rumblings and peals of thunder." These are indicative of God's power, and bring to mind his appearance at Sinai.

"Before the throne, seven lamps were blazing. These are the seven spirits of God. And before the throne there was what looked like a sea of glass, clear as crystal." The *seven spirits* are indicative of divine perfection. The remaining symbolism seemingly expands on this notion.

In the center, around the throne, were four seraphs (cf. Isa 6:1–2). Day and night, they proclaim: "Holy, holy, holy is the Lord God Almighty,

---

6. Mounce, *The Book of Revelation*, 65–66.

7. Wall, *op. cit.*, 89.

who was, and is, and is to come." At this, the twenty-four elders prostrate themselves before the throne, and declare: "You are worthy, our Lord and God, to receive glory and honor and power, for you created all things, and by your will they were created and have their being." In this regard, they echo the adoration expressed by the angelic creatures.

Since God is *holy*, he will not tolerate the degradation that permeates life. In particular, *Babylon* is singled out for reproach. While the symbolism is derived from the Babylonian captivity, Rome appears to be the culprit. Especially grievous was the idolatry associated with emperor worship.

Another angel makes its appearance. "He had great authority, and the earth was illuminated by his splendor" (18:1). Whereupon, he shouted with a loud voice: "Fallen! Fallen is Babylon the Great! For all the nations have drunk the maddening wine of her adulteries."

Then John heard another voice from heaven saying: "Come out of her, my people, so that you will not share in her sins, so that you will not receive any of her plagues, for her sins are piled up to heaven, and God has remembered her crimes." After that, the lament continues.

John then heard what sounded like a great multitude in heaven shouting: "Hallelujah! Salvation and glory and power belong to our God, for true and just are his judgments." Thus, hope and justice again appear in consort with one another.

Moreover, John saw a new heaven and earth, for the first had passed away (21:1). This final apocalyptic segment describes "the new Jerusalem adorned as a bride for her husband, the new order in which sorrow will be no more, the eternal city resplendent with gold and precious stone, and the incredible joy of God's servant, who will finally 'see his face.'"[8]

In this connection, "the angel showed me the river of the water of life, as clear as crystal, flowing from the throne of God and of the Lamb down the middle of the great street of the city" (22:1–2). On each side of the river stood the tree of life, bearing fruit all year around. "No longer will there be any curse. The throne of God and the Lamb will be in the city, and his servants will serve him." In proverbial terms, "There is no greater honor than to serve in a great cause."

As noted above, they will see his face. "Blessed are the pure in heart," Jesus observed, "for they will see God" (Matt 5:8). In addition, his name

---

8. Mounce, *op. cit.*, 379.

would be written on their foreheads. Accordingly, "The faces of those who have experienced the beatific vision will reflect the unmistakable likeness of their heavenly Father. The process of transformation now under way in the life of the believer will be brought to completion which the church enters its ultimate and ideal state."[9]

Furthermore, "There will be no more night." There will be no need for a lamp or the light of the sun, "for the Lord God will give them light." As if an eternal benediction.

"These things are trustworthy and true," the angel assures John. One does not hope in vain.

It remains to act in accord with our prospect for the future. "Behold, I am coming soon!" Jesus alerts the reader. "Blessed is he who keeps the words of the prophecy in this book." The return of the Lord in glory is imminent, especially in that it could occur at any moment, and moreover in that the Messianic Age has dawned. Hence, one should not procrastinate nor despair.

"The Spirit and the bride say, 'Come!' And let him who hears say, 'Come!' Whoever is thirsty, let him come; and whoever wishes, let him take the free gift of the water of life." "Amen. Come Lord Jesus. The grace of the Lord Jesus be with God's people." It consequently bears repeating: such as sustain a vibrant hope, in keeping with divine justice, and labor with righteous resolve.

---

9. Ibid., 400.

6

JUSTICE AND LOVE

LOVE ROUNDS OUT THE TRIAD OF THEOLOGICAL/SPIRITUAL VIRTUES. In that love "does not delight in evil, but rejoices with the truth" (1 Cor 13:6), we would gather that it advocates justice. Nothing worthwhile is calculated to be gained through deceit or pretense.

A certain scribe inquired of Jesus, "Teacher, which is the greatest commandment in the Law?" (Matt 22:35). It was sometimes argued that all commandments were equally obligatory, since the violating of any was a breach of the covenant. The rabbis also said that by being observant of more trivial concerns one was less likely to violate some more substantial matter. Also, they speculated that it was more pious to keep an objectionable regulation than an alternative. As a result, we can readily see that it was a topic that would not be laid to rest.

Along this line, a rabbi posed the rhetorical question: "What is wrong with building fences?" Since it was supposed that in keeping the finer points of the law one was less likely to be tempted. When I deferred to him for an answer, he replied: "Nothing is wrong with building fences, so long as one does not worship them." Worship is reserved for the Almighty, and all else amounts to idolatry.

In any case, Jesus responded: "'Love the Lord your God with all your heart and with all your soul and with all your mind.' And the second is like it: 'Love your neighbor as yourself.' All the Law and the Prophets hang on these two commandments." As for the former, the *Shema* (derived from *hear*) constitutes the foundation for Jewish thought. As for the latter, "For anyone who does not love his brother, whom he has seen, cannot love God, whom he has not seen" (1 John 4:20). Since the one is evidence of the other.

Moreover, "We love because he first loved us" (v. 19). It is in reflecting on God's love for us that incites us to love him in return. "It is, therefore, good for us constantly to renew our knowledge of God's love as we read of it in the Bible, as we hear it proclaimed in the worship of the church, and as we consider the ways in which our whole life has been molded by experiences of God's love and care for us."[1]

As prime evidence of God's abiding love, "For God so loved the world that he gave his one and only Son, that whoever believes in him shall not perish but have eternal life" (John 3:16). Charles Wesley was perhaps the most prolific hymn writer of all time. Following his conversion, he is reported to have composed an average of two hymns every week for fifty years. In the above connection, he wrote:

> And can it be that I should gain
> An interest in the Savior's blood?
> Died He for me, who cause His pain?
> For me, who Him to death pursued?
> Amazing love! How can it be
> That Thou, my Lord, shouldst die for me?

In greater detail, "Your attitude should be the same as that of Christ Jesus" (Phil 2:6). "Who, being in very nature God, did not consider equality with God something to be grasped, but made himself nothing, taking the very nature of a servant, being made in human likeness." He voluntarily exchanged his role of sovereign to servant for no other reason than his compassion for the lost.

"And being found in appearance as a man, he humbled himself and became obedient to death—even death on a cross!" It is difficult for us, "after so many Christian centuries during which the cross has been venerated as a sacred symbol, to realize the unspeakable horror and disgust that the mention or indeed the very thought of the cross invoked. In polite Roman society the word 'cross' was an obscenity, not to be uttered in conversation."[2]

---

1. Marshall, *The Epistles of John*, 225
2. Bruce, *Philippians*, 71.

Even so, it is in keeping with the thrust of the passage—since it graphically illustrates the extent to which love will go to accomplish its purpose. Thus, should one be tempted by the exigencies of life to question God's compassion, he or she need only recall the cross by way of assurance. In other words, the cross casts an exceedingly long shadow.

For this reason, he was highly exalted, and given a name above all others—"that at the name of Jesus every knee should bow, in heaven and on earth and under the earth, and every tongue confess that Jesus Christ is Lord, to the glory of God the Father." In this regard, he receives that which he rightly deserves.

Jesus explores the topic further in a memorable parable. A scribe inquired of him, "Teacher, what must I do to inherit eternal life?" (Luke 10:25). The question assumes that while salvation is a divine prerogative persons must be cooperative.

"What is written in the Law?" Jesus countered. "How do you read it?" In other words, how do you interpret its teaching?

He responded as had Jesus on the above occasion, "'Love the Lord your God with all your heart and with all your soul and with all your strength and with all your mind' and 'Love your neighbor as yourself.'"

"You have answered correctly," Jesus commended him. "Do this and you shall live." It goes without saying that this is easier said than done.

Accordingly and wanting to justify himself, he inquired: "And who is my neighbor?" In response, Jesus told a story concerning a man who was going down from Jerusalem to Jericho—when accosted by thieves who left him *half dead*. A priest happened to come along, and viewing the stricken man, passed by on the other side of the road. He perhaps felt it was dangerous to get involved.

So also, a Levite came along, and he too passed by on the other side. Both he and the priest may have thought they had other pressing duties that took precedent. Moreover, motives are as a rule mixed.

A Samaritan now made his appearance. In Jewish tradition, Samaritans were depreciated as *lion converts*. It seems that the king of Assyria resettled the region with pagans from elsewhere. "When they first lived there, they did not worship the Lord, so he sent lions among them and they killed some of the people" (2 Kings 17:25). When this was reported to the Assyrian ruler, he mandated: "Have one of the priests you took captive from Samaria go back to live there and teach the people what the god of the land requires." This was perceived as a matter of expediency, quite lacking in pious devotion.

His bad reputation notwithstanding, the Samaritan took pity on the injured person. He bandaged up the man's wounds, put him on his donkey, and brought him to an inn. There he arranged for the man's needs. Initially making a down payment and promising to pay any remainder upon his return. "Which of these three do you think was a neighbor to the man who fell into the hands of robbers?" Jesus pointedly inquired.

"The one who had mercy on him," the scribe replied.

"Go and do likewise," Jesus then admonished him. It turns out that one's neighbor is anyone we befriend. Thus, while love provides the impetus, justice is served.

We turn next to a curious episode in which two words translate as *love*: *agape* and *philos*. "Simon, son of John, do you truly love (*agape*) me more than these?" Jesus inquired (John 21:13). *These* was perhaps a reference to the others, or possibly the means by which the apostle had earned his living.

"Yes, Lord," he said, "you know that I love (*philos*) you."

Jesus replied, "Feed my lambs."

Again Jesus asked, "Simon son of John, do you truly love (*agape*) me?" When he answered to the affirmative (employing *philos*), Jesus enjoined him: "Take care of my sheep." Then for the third time Jesus inquired, "Simon son of John, do you love (shifting to *philos*) do you love me?"

Peter was hurt because Jesus had inquired three times, as if to question his sincerity and/or resolve. "Lord," he protested, "you know all things; you know that I love (*philos*) you."

Jesus then admonished him: "Feed my sheep." Consequently, his willingness to minister to Jesus' followers appears as evidence of genuine love.

Commentators are not agreed as to what to make of this play on words. Some think it no more than a literary device, while others think there is more at stake. As for the latter, there are four words to take into consideration. "*Storge* is the least familiar. It focuses on filial devotions. It calls attention to the love parents feel for and express toward their children, the appreciative response of their children, and the relationship between and among siblings."[3]

This, in turn, recalls a Bedouin proverb: "Me against my cousin, and my cousin and I against the stranger." Or as I was reminded as a child, "Blood is thicker than water." Actually, I did not have to be convinced that family was special.

Eros has a sexual connotation. In this regard: "How beautiful you are, my darling! Oh, how beautiful! Your eyes behind your veil are doves. Your hair is like a flock of goats descending from Mount Gilead" (Song of Songs 4:1). The beloved replies: "Awake, north wind, and come south wind! Blow on my garden, that its fragrance may spread abroad. Let my lover come into his garden and taste its choice fruits."

Their relationship hinges on the complementary character of the couple. Each contributes something lacking in the other. As a result, both are fulfilled. On the other hand, neither should be reduced to simply an object for sexual gratification.

Philos draws upon a relationship between or among persons engaged in a common activity. The Greeks notably applied it to those sharing an academic pursuit. However, we are more likely to think in terms of team sports. Bonds formed in this context are calculated to endure into later life.

"A friend loves at all time," the sage allows, "and a brother is born for adversity" (Prov 17:17). In proverbial terms, "A friend in need is a friend indeed!" Even so, we are admonished to not impose on our friendship.

Finally, *agape* is employed to characterize God's unconditional love, and that of those who emulate him. This is not to suggest that he is necessarily approving of our behavior. Otherwise expressed, this amounts to *hard love*—thought to be ideally present in parents but often lacking in grandparents.

In practical terms, "The worldly man treats certain people kindly because he 'likes' them; the Christian, trying to treat every one kindly, finds himself liking more and more peoples as he goes on—including people he would not even have imagined himself liking at the beginning."[4]

Agape thus differs from the rest, in that it is expressed gratuitously. Accordingly, Jesus initially inquires as to unconditional love, but in the

---

3. .Inch, *Why Take the Bible Seriously?*, 62.
4. Lewis, *Mere Christianity*, 114.

last instance reverts to a lesser allegiance. Conversely, Peter appears restrained throughout—perhaps out of deference to his earlier denial.

It remains to explore Paul's *most excellent way*. In this regard, he concludes his discussion of spiritual gifts with a crescendo of rhetorical questions. "Are all apostles?" (1 Cor 12:29). Manifestly not! "Are all prophets?" Certainly not! "Are all teachers?" Not as usually understood. "Do all work miracles?" Only in select instances. "Do all have gifts of healing?" Obviously not. "Do all speak in tongues?" Apparently not. "Do all interpret?" Not in any given instance.

Therefore, it is that the corporate fellowship benefits from constructive diversity, which is essential to unity. Conversely, conformity receives a failing grade. Nor is there any place for boasting, since it is the Spirit who endows persons for their ministry.

"But eagerly desire the greater gifts." Such as will edify the fellowship. Not those that create divisions and discontent. Depending on the more pressing needs, perhaps not even the same gifts on any given occasion. "And now I will show you the most excellent way," the apostle adds.

Paul then elaborates on the preeminent role of *love* in fostering Christian fellowship. It results "in a passage of singular beauty and power. He has not finished with the 'gifts', and he has much to say about them in the following chapter. But, it is integral to his argument that the central thing is not the due exercise of any of the 'gifts'. It is love."[5] For which there is no genuine substitute.

In greater detail, "If I speak in the tongues of men and angels, but have not love, I am only a resounding gong or a clanging cymbal" (13:1). Whether or not he has in mind speaking in tongues, "the expression is general enough to cover speech of any kind. No language in earth or heaven is to be compared with the practice of life. It is easy enough to be fascinated by eloquent discourse, to be hypnotized by the magic of words, and to pass over that which matters most of all."[6]

In this connection, a polished sermon is not necessarily a public service. One can go to great lengths in order to make a good impression, and be quite lacking in compassion. Lacking love, one does not actually speak the truth.

---

5. Morris, *I Corinthians*, 176.
6. Ibid.

"If I have the gift of prophecy and can fathom all mysteries and all knowledge, and I have a faith that can move mountains, but have not love, I am nothing." Accordingly, it would appear that those who speculate on the end times could put their efforts to better purpose. By way of reminder, "We learn in order to do."

Furthermore, *a faith that can move mountains* appears to be idiomatic. Since they appear impervious to circumstances, and resistant to our efforts. Consequently, only a superlative faith would alter their configuration. Even then, without love, it amounts to nothing.

"If I give all I possess to the poor and surrender my body to the flames," the apostle continues, "but have not love, I gain nothing." While generosity is commended, it should be properly motivated. In particular, in order to glorify God and render a genuine service—rather than seek the acclaim of others.

Even martyrdom can be self-seeking. In contrast, Ignatius earnestly writes: "For though I desire to suffer, yet I know not whether I am worthy; for the envy of the devil is unseen indeed by many, but against me it wages the fiercer war. So then I crave gentleness, whereby the prince of this world is brought to nought."[7]

The apostle thereupon sets out to characterize *love*. Initially, "Love is patient, love is kind, it does not envy, it does not boast, it is not proud." It thus takes into consideration that we are all works in progress. In this regard, it treats others as we would have them treat us. This extends to being kind, rather than inconsiderate. It, moreover, is not given to pride, which fails to appreciate how much we are indebted to others—God, family, and friends.

Elaborated further, love "is not rude, it is not self-seeking, it is not easily angered, it keeps no record of wrongs." As noted in an earlier context, it is *civil*. As such, it extends to "Saying 'please' and 'thank you'; lowering our voice whenever it may threaten or interfere with others' tranquility; raising funds for a neighborhood renovation program; acknowledging a new-comer to the conversation; listening to understand and help," and the like.[8]

"Love does not delight in evil but rejoices with the truth. It always protects, always trusts, always hopes, always perseveres." It is an advocate

---

7. Ignatius, *To the Trallians*, 4
8. Forni, *op. cit.*, 9.

of justice. Not simply for the privileged of society, but also the oppressed. Not to be acclaimed by man, but commended by the Almighty. Along with a persisting resolve, that will not be dissuaded by opposition, circumstances, or weariness.

"Love never fails. But where there are prophecies, they will cease; where there are tongues, they will be stilled; where there is knowledge, it will pass away. For we know in part and we prophesy in part, but when perfection comes, the imperfect disappears."

Accordingly, love is triumphant even in death. In this connection, Tertullian affirms: "The more often we are mown down by you, the more in number we grow. The blood of Christians is seed."[9]

The contrast between the partial and perfection is illustrated from the human life. When I was a child, I talked like a child, I thought like a child, I reasoned like a child. When I became a man I put childish ways behind me. As one matures, love takes on added significance.

"Now we see but a poor reflection as in a mirror, then we shall see face to face. Now I know in part; then I shall know fully, even as I am fully known." The more we know, the more we realize we do not know. This resembles seeing one's image in a bronze mirror. While a poor reflection, it is one with which we must be content for the present.

"And now these three remain: faith, hope and love. But the greatest of these is love." As things stand, we are left to weigh three eternal verities. These will stand us in good stead, in this life and the life to come. Also, when material things have lost much of their appeal.

"Do not store up for yourselves treasures on earth, where moth and rust destroy, and where thieves break in and steal," Jesus accordingly admonished. "But store up for yourselves treasures in heaven, where moth and rust do not destroy, and where thieves do not break in and steal. For where your treasure is, there your heart will be also" (Matt 6:19–21). This was by way of assessing our priorities.

Of these three, *love* receives the prime commendation. In this regard, "Whoever does not love does not know God, because God is love" (1 John 4:8). Love and justice thus prove to be highly compatible, and indeed necessary in the pursuit of virtue.

---

9. Tertullian, *The Apology*, L.

7

COMMUTATIVE JUSTICE

JUSTICE MAKES AN APPEARANCE IN A WIDE RANGE OF SITUATIONS. One of those touched on in passing has to do with the transfer of goods and services, designated as *commutative justice*. Consequently, it is something with which most are familiar.

Initially, this recalls my father as the proprietor of a village store, involved primarily with the sale of groceries. He had passed up a sport's scholarship to assist my grandfather, and inherited the business. His was one of two local enterprises.

Dad put in long hours. During the winter months, this entailed rising early and building a fire in the furnace. Upon returning well into the evening, he wasted little time in making his way to the bedroom. Closed on Sunday, Dad would open only to accommodate persons who needed his service.

He had an assistant when able to afford one. Otherwise, Dad managed alone. He charged what he thought was a fair price, although he could not compete with the chain stores, which dealt in larger quantities.

Folk often took advantage of him. When allowed to charge their purchases, they were often reluctant to reimburse him. Instead, they would often drive out of town for purchases and recreation. Then, when hard pressed, they would plead with him to *put it on the tab*.

How well was justice served? It is hard to say, since persons expect to have a fair return on their labors. When depressed with his lot in life, my father would on occasion refer to the store as his *jail*. By way of clarification, he was seldom happier than when making his way through some wooded area. It was then, according to his report, that he felt closest to God.

Now "The Lord God took the man and put him in the Garden of Eden to work it and take care of it" (Gen 2:15). Labor is thus depicted as a given. Accordingly, the rabbis reasoned that if a person slacked off during the week, he could not properly observe the Sabbath. Incidentally, this does not give him cause to ravage his environment.

There was yet no division of labor, which would come in due time. Still, labor appears as a critical ingredient, meant to be shared. It was illustrated by one of my mother's favorite expressions, "Take a load when you go." While explicitly related to stacking our dirty dishes, it intended broader application.

As vinegar to the teeth and smoke to the eyes, so is a sluggard to those who send him" (Prov 10:26). Both analogies mean to express disapproval of those who shirk their responsibilities. In other words, they are an irritant to society.

"The sluggard craves and gets nothing, but the desires of the diligent are fully satisfied" (Prov 13:4). Here the indolent is set over against a conscientious person. As for the former, his or her desires remain unmet. As for the latter, he or she is appreciatively satisfied.

"The sluggard says, 'There is lion in the road, a fierce lion roaming streets!' As a door turns on its hinges, so a sluggard turns on his bed. The sluggard buries his hand in the dish; he is too lazy to bring it back to his mouth" (Prov 26:13–15). The point is that he will devise any excuse, no matter how unreasonable, to idle away his time.

Qualifications aside, it is good to be gainfully employed. Commutative justice is thereby served, as persons make a constructive contribution to society. It likewise builds self-esteem.

Commutative justice first makes its appearance with reference to Cain and Abel. "Now Abel kept flocks, and Cain worked the soil" (Gen 4:2). "The first brothers developed two different professions. Abel became a shepherd, Cain a farmer. This raises the question whether the conflict between Cain and Abel is between two brothers or a class conflict between two different ways of life."[1] Perhaps both.

In any case, their vocations appear in context of the family. This was in keeping with the culture of the time. Then, too, it continued to linger

---

1. Hartley, *op.cit.*, 80.

in many instances—as with my father. However, by this time, alternatives were more available. In this connection, my father considered leaving the family business and taking a better paying position in a lumber mill. Family ties, however, proved stronger than lucrative returns.

One can readily imagine that the siblings would have cultivated different perspectives concerning commutative justice. Such would value the labor associated with one's own vocation over that of the other. This disparity likely increased with the passing of time, as each attempted to make his case.

Conversely, the text gives the impression that one vocation is not intrinsically preferable to the other. Except for natural attributes, since some take to one line of work better than to another. Then, in terms of the family, the diversity provides alternative means of income. This proves to be particularly helpful during times of famine or other natural disasters.

"In the course of time Cain brought some of the fruits of the soil as an offering to the Lord. But Abel brought fat portions from some of the firstborn of his flock." Accordingly, the Lord looked with favor on Abel's offering, but not that of Cain. As for the former, it resembled a choice portion one would lay before an honored guest. As for the latter, it amounted to a token exercise.

Commutative justice also has religious connotations. This was implied in the giving of the *tithe* (tenth), which was largely levied for maintaining religious activities. In this regard, the sage admonishes: "Honor the Lord with your wealth, with the firstfruits of all your crops; then your barns will be filled to overflowing, and your vats will brim over with new wine" (Prov 3:9).

In keeping with this concern, the rabbis were convinced that if one would cheat God, he would not be reluctant to cheat others. Thus, commutative justice starts to unravel when ignoring one's covenant obligations. In a manner of speaking, "Give God his due, and life begins to fall into place." Otherwise, even our sincere efforts fall considerably short.

So Cain was exceedingly angry. He no doubt thought he deserved better as the elder brother. "Why are you angry?" the Lord inquired. "If you do what is right, will you not be accepted? But if you do not do what is right, sin is crouching at your door; it desires to have you, but you must master it." Sin is thus depicted as a wild beast, waiting to pounce on its victim. Unless tamed, it will surely succeed.

"Let's go out in the field," Cain proposed to his sibling. While they were in the field, Cain attacked and killed Abel.

"Where is your brother Abel?" the Lord inquired of Cain.

"I don't know," he replied. "Am I my brother's keeper?" Given his sarcastic response, Cain repudiates the responsibility an elder brother customarily accords to his younger sibling. Needless to say, members of one's family do not frequent cages.

The Lord apparently did not think that Cain's question deserved a reply. "What have you done?" he countered. "Listen! Your brother's blood cries out to me from the ground. When you work the ground, it will no longer yield its crops to you. You will be a restless wanderer on the earth." "The wandering nomadic lifestyle to which Cain is doomed represents one of the principal economic/social divisions in ancient society. Once animals had been domesticated, around 8000 B. C., herding and pastoral nomadism became a major economic pursuit for tribes and villages."[2]

These herdsmen followed migration routes, which as a rule provided water and grazing for their animals. From time to time, they clashed with village folk—over access to needed resources. In proverbial terms, "Might makes right."

It was not an enviable prospect. In particular, Cain feared that someone would take vengeance on him for the slaying of his brother. "Not so," the Lord assured him. "Then the Lord put a mark on Cain so that no one who found him would kill him." It is an obscure reference, which served to protect Cain from retaliation.

We subsequently read that Jacob upon arriving in the vicinity of Shechem pitched his tent within sight of the city. "For a hundred pieces of silver, he bought from the sons of Hamor the plot of ground where he had pitched his tent" (Gen. 33:19). As with Abraham before him, he purchased this property as an earnest of the promised land.

This would involve various social amenities. For instance, one would suppose that he indicated his intent by initially pitching his tent. This initiative could be rejected, provided that there was no implied coercion, and the conditions for sale were acceptable. Then, in addition, the agreement would act as a social contract, providing additional security for the participants.

---

2. Walton and Matthews, *op. cit.*, 22.

In another instance, the Lord instructed David to build an altar on the threshing floor of Araunah the Jebusite. When Araunah saw David and his attendants approaching, he bowed before the king out of deference. "Why has my lord the king come to his servant?" he inquired (2 Sam 24:21).

"To buy your threshing floor," David answered, "so I can build an altar to the Lord, that the plague on the people may be stopped." The threshing floor would have been located on an elevated location, making it a desirable place to erect an altar.

"Let my lord the king take whatever pleases him and offer it up. Here are oxen for the burnt offering, and here are threshing sledges and ox yokes for the wood." Whereupon, he petitioned: "May the Lord your God accept you." "The story forms a parallel to that of Abraham's purchase of a burial site in Genesis 23. In both instances the proposal to provide freely what was requested is part of the bargaining procedure rather than a serious offer."[3]

"No," David protested, "I insist on paying you for it. I will not sacrifice to the Lord my God burnt offerings that cost me nothing." Otherwise expressed, it would constitute a violation of commutative justice. Accordingly, he paid fifty shekels of silver for the threshing floor and the oxen. He built the altar, offered the sacrifice, and the plague terminated.

Along a related line, slavery was widespread in the ancient Near East—although the economy was not necessarily dependent on it. Conversely, it was said that about half the persons in the Roman Empire were slaves early in the Christian era. These could be purchased from their owners, merchants, as prisoners of war, or simply to pay off their debt. "If a fellow Hebrew, a man or a woman, sells himself to you and serves you six years, in the seventh year you must let him go free. And when you release him, do not send him away empty-handed. Supply him liberally from your flock, your threshing floor, and your winepress" (Deut 15:14). Especially in the light of their own recollections of being in bondage.

Accordingly, the Genesis narrative appears as if an emancipation proclamation. So it was that the Hebrews were reminded that so long as anyone is in bondage, no one is genuinely free.

Of course, slavery exists in subtle forms. As when the markets are so manipulated to require that persons work inordinately long hours, with

---

3. Evans, *1 and 2 Samuel*, 247–248.

modest remuneration. Then under duress, so that one is driven to the brink of despair.

Moreover, commutative justice requires that we give attention to detail. In this regard, "You must have accurate and honest weights and measures, so that you may live long in the land the Lord your God is giving you" (Deut 25:15). "Fair trade is one of the essential hallmarks of any human society seeking to protect everybody's interest in a civilized way. There is, on the one hand, the positive promise that commitment to honesty will bring the covenant blessing."[4] There is, on the other, the warning that dishonesty is *detestable* to the Lord.

I recall an Arab antiquities dealer—who took meticulous care not to misrepresent his merchandise. So much so, that he would settle for a more recent date if in doubt. His reputation for honesty was thus well deserved.

"If a slave has taken refuge with you, do not hand him over to his master. Let him live among you wherever he likes and in whatever town he chooses. Do not oppress him" (Deut 23:15–16). "That is, the legal rights and expectations intrinsic to slavery as a social institution are subordinated to the rights of the slave as a human being with needs. Thus, the legal right to hold property in the form of persons (slaves) is not abolished, but it is certainly relativized and subordinated."[5]

This brings to mind the importance of *extenuating circumstances* in the pursuit of commutative justice. In particular, what are the options? Also, what are the anticipated results? Finally, what can be done to correct any miscalculations?

This, moreover, was one that preyed on human vulnerability. As such, it is not in principle unlike the appeal to legalize gambling for some worthwhile project. Both alike tend to have an adverse domino effect on society.

Shifting focus: "Do not charge your brother interest, whether on money or food or anything else that may earn interest. You may charge a foreigner interest, but not a brother Israelite." Once again, this stipulation stands in marked contrast to surrounding ancient Near Eastern countries, where it was common to charge high interest rates.

---

4. Wright, *op. cit.*, 267.
5. Ibid., 250.

In particular, this is in anticipation of settlement in the promised land. It would require a corporate effort, in keeping with their covenant obligations. However, while they could charge foreigners interest, it was not obligatory that they do so. Commutative justice can thus be seen to play out differently from one setting to another.

The people are also cautioned: "If you make a vow to the Lord your God, do not be slow to pay it, for the Lord your God will certainly demand it of you and you will be guilty of sin. But if you refrain from making a vow, you will not be guilty." Accordingly, the sage observes: "It is a trap for a man to dedicate something rashly and only later to consider his vows" (Prov 20:25).

This, moreover, recalls the proverbial saying: "Act in haste, and repent at leisure." In more detail, Jesus inquired: "Suppose one of you wants to build a tower. Will he not first sit down and estimate the cost to see if he has enough money to complete it? For if he lays the foundation and is not able to finish it, everyone who sees it will ridicule him" (Luke 14:28–29).

Now if one enters his neighbor's vineyard, he may eat as many of the grapes as he desires, "but do not put any in your basket. If you enter your neighbor's grainfield, you may pick kernel with your hands, but you must not put a sickle to the standing grain." "Neighborly should allow a hungry traveler to have something to eat from one's crops without charge or grudge. On the other hand, this ancient privilege should not be abused by actions tantamount to theft."[6]

"Of what use is money in the hand of a fool," the sage inquires, "since he has no desire to get wisdom?" (Prov 17:16). *Wisdom* pertains to the application of knowledge. I remember a time when I was having lunch in the school cafeteria with the provocative clinical psychologist Don Tweedie. A student stopped by our table to inquire about the selection of an academic major. Tweedie, who was known for his unexpected observation, replied: "It doesn't much matter. Find a professor who has insight into life and learn all you can from him or her." Welcome to the realm of wisdom?

This vividly contrasts with a friend who in jest asserts, "The one with the most toys wins." Such as the materialist, who gathers much but saves nothing.

---

6. Ibid., 253.

"'It's no good, it's no good,' says the buyer; then off he goes and boasts about his purchase" (Prov 20:14). "This is a somewhat humorous observation about purchasing. The charm lies in the contrast between the two scenes: undervaluing the object, and the boast of the bargain. This observation is true of ancient bartering and modern sales."[7]

In conclusion, commutative justice takes on a metaphorical usage. "Do you not know that your body is a temple of the Holy Spirit, who is in you, whom you have received from God?" Paul rhetorically inquires. "You are not your own, you were bought at a price. Therefore honor God with your body" (1 Cor 6:19–20). The apostle seems incredulous. Surely, they must be aware of the transaction!

In particular, they have been purchased at a great cost. As a result, the Holy Spirit has taken possession. Consequently, they are to present themselves as servants of righteousness, rather than slaves of sin.

While continuing the same line of reasoning, Paul makes a different application: "You who were bought with a price; do not become slaves of men"—recalling the earlier discussion of slavery. "Brothers, each man, as responsible to God, should remain in the situation God called him to" (1 Cor 23–24). In whatever situation one finds him or herself, one is to render diligent service as unto the Lord.

Then should there be a conflict of interest, one is obligated to the higher power. One is not meant to compromise legitimate convictions. Nor is one expected to simply comply with the requirements, but go beyond them in selfless service.

Then, by way of caution, do not emulate the false prophets. Such "will secretly introduce destructive heresies, even denying the sovereign Lord who bought them—bringing swift destruction on themselves" (2 Peter 2:1). Whether in this instance or some other, they tend to disregard the implications of commutative justice.

---

7. Murphy and Huwiler, *Proverbs, Ecclesiastes, Song of Songs*, 100.

8

Distributive Justice

John Kennedy's memorable appeal, "Ask not what the country can do for you, but what you can do for your country" is vintage *distributive justice*. Accordingly, "Distributive justice regulates the measure of privileges, aids, burdens or charges, and obligations of the individual as a member of the community."[1] A person exercises distributive justice when assuming a legitimate obligation for society, while not insisting on excessive privileges.

Now certain of the Pharisees determined to entrap Jesus. They sent delegates along with Herodians to accomplish their purpose. The latter apparently "supported the family of Herod and had a vested interest in the maintenance of peace and the status quo in Palestine. These Herodians and disciples of the Pharisees approach Jesus with complimentary words . . . as a deliberate attempt to incline Jesus from the start to an answer that might incriminate him."[2]

"Teacher," they observed, "we know you are a man of integrity and that you teach the way of God in accordance with the truth. You are not swayed by man, because you pay no attention to who they are.

Tell us then, what is your opinion? Is it right to pay taxes to Caesar or not?" (Matt 22:16–17).

Should he reply negatively, they supposed he would lose popular support. Should he respond positively, he might be charged with inciting a revolt. It was from their perspective a win/win situation.

---

1. Haring, *op. cit.*, vol. 1, 517.
2. Hagner, *Matthew 14–28*, 635.

Jesus being aware of their evil intent, inquired: "You hypocrites, why are you trying to trap me? Show me the coin used for paying the tax." When they brought him a denarius, he inquired further: "Whose portrait is this? And whose inscription?"

"Caesar's," they replied.

Then he said to them, "Give to Caesar what is Caesar's, and to God what is God's." When they heard his counsel, they were amazed and went their way—having been frustrated in their attempt to snare him.

The appropriateness of Jesus' response appears evident. Initially, there are obligations associated with being a member of society—evidenced by the paying of taxes. The funds gathered serve a number of legitimate purposes, such as providing security, the building of roads, and a variety of essential services.

Unfortunately, it does not guarantee that the funds will be conscientiously administered. For instance, one must always face the prospect of an expanding public bureaucracy—as if it were an end in itself. Then, too, resources may be drained off to satisfy the greed of special interest groups.

In any case, one can exercise only a limited control over how his or her taxes are distributed. This will differ from one society to the next, and some will be more capable of initiating constructive change than others. Moreover, cooperative efforts are more likely of success than strictly individual initiatives.

We would also conclude that the realms of Caesar and God are not altogether independent of one another. In this regard, "Everyone must submit himself to the governing authorities, for there is no authority except that which God has established. Consequently, he who rebels against the authority is rebelling against what God has instituted, and those who do so will bring judgment on themselves" (Rom 13:1–2).

While Christians are not the only people subject to the public officials, it is especially incumbent on them that they recognize the authority structure is ordained of God. It is understood that this does not condone all that transpires concerning governance. There is, in fact, a higher court of appeal that must be taken into consideration.

"You are the salt of the earth," Jesus observed. "But if the salt loses its saltiness, how can it be made salty again? It is no longer good for anything, except to be thrown out and trampled by men" (Matt 5:13). The designation *you* is corporate, referring to the Christian fellowship. "In the immediate context Jesus seems to be saying that those who live out the qualities listed in the Beatitudes will permeate the world and retard its moral and ethical decay."[3]

Should the community lose its essential ingredient, it would no longer serve in its intended capacity. In greater detail, this may take the form of a consensus. However, the church must bear in mind that it cannot pontificate in matters that are not expressly set forth in Holy Writ. Thus while the sanctity of life should be of general concern, actual legislation may be subject to differences of opinion.

Christians may through para-church agencies take on causes that are more explicit. These are not calculated to speak on behalf of the Christian community as such, but those of like conviction—as informed by their faith. As a result, these provide a more aggressive means of social involvement.

Christians may also join with others in some worthwhile cause not distinctively associated with the corporate fellowship. These are said to involve people of *good will*, regardless of religious orientation. We are thus encouraged to entertain creative means for social betterment.

Then, finally, the individual may embrace a social initiative—with or without the help of others. I recall a college student weighing the prospects of urban youth ministry. He solicited my appraisal for a novel model he had devised. While lacking the credentials to evaluate his venture adequately, I was greatly impressed with his project.

It bears repeating, "Give to Caesar what is Caesar's, and to God what is God's." As for the former, to exercise *distributive justice*. As for the latter, to do so within in the constraints of God's sovereign rule over the affairs of humans.

In greater detail, we will touch on three provocative essays generated by the Evangelical Theological Society's Washington Convention (1993)—published under the appropriate title *God and Caesar*. Daniel Estes allows at the outset of his discussion: "Contemporary American society faces a crises of leadership. The questions raised by Watergate, Iran-Contra and White Water linger on. Trust and respect for politicians and political institutions remains mired at the bottom of public opinion polls."[4]

---

3. Mounce, *Matthew*, 42.
4. Estes, *God and Caesar*, 7.

He subsequently turns to Psalm 101 for its perspective on a political leadership calculated to inspire trust. "I will sing of your love and justice; to you, O Lord, I will sing praise" (101:1). It is out of his personal devotion to the Lord that he determines to emulate his ways. This is explicitly expressed in terms of *love* and *justice*. Not as a begrudging duty, but as an act of worship.

"I will be careful to lead a blameless life—when will you come to me?" "In modern language it speaks of integrity, the seamless quality which unites a person's entire life—attitudes, ambitions, actions—by one central focus. (This) supersedes the convenient dichotomy between one's private life and public life. Instead, the person is viewed holistically."[5] Then, realizing his personal inadequacy, the psalmist calls on the Lord for assistance.

In greater detail, "I will set before my eyes no vile thing. The deeds of faithless men I hate; they will not cling to me; I will have nothing to do with evil." In proverbial terms, he draws a line in the sand. As a result, he will wage a relentless warfare against all that is seductively evil.

In the second half of the psalm, its author deftly moves the emphasis from his personal integrity to public conduct. In particular, he identifies those with whom he will choose to associate. "Whoever slanders his neighbor in secret, him will I put to silence; whoever has haughty eyes and a proud heart, him will I not endure." Since these will prove a distraction from his righteous resolve.

Conversely, "My eyes will be on the faithful in the land, that they may dwell with me; he whose walk is blameless will minister to me." In that they will prove to be a righteous influence, and faithful mentors. A faithful guide is to be desired more than material riches.

Continuing the contrast, "No one who practices deceit will dwell in my house; and one who speaks falsely will stand in my presence." Truth is too valuable a commodity to be compromised. Cherish the truth, reflect on the truth, speak the truth, and live according to what is true. For, as expressed by Augustine, "All truth is God's truth."

Then in conclusion, "Every morning I will put to silence all the wicked in the land; I will cut off every evildoer from the city of the Lord." The psalmist thus allows that as a political official he has a constant obligation to affirm rectitude acceptable to the Almighty, and beneficial to the

---

5. Ibid., 13–14.

populace. Qualifications aside, the principles involved here are applicable to the contemporary American situation.

D. Jeffry Bingham contributes the second essay, by way of suggesting that the enterprise of the church in the early centuries provides a valuable resource for pressing problems associated with contemporary society. In particular, he opts to reflect on Irenaeus' polemic work *Adversus Haereses* in this connection.

As a relevant aside, Irenaeus was one of the more articulate of the early church fathers. Of his extensive writings, only two survive: *Proof of the Apostolic Teaching* and the before mentioned work. The latter takes the form of a sprawling attack on Gnosticism, summarizing its teachings and contrasting them to orthodox instruction.

Irenaeus proceeds to take issue with the devil's claim that all the kingdoms of the world have been given to him, to do with as he pleases (cf. Luke 4:5–6). He notes in this regard, "the heart of the king is in the hand of God" (Prov 21:1). In addition, "By me kings reign, and the mighty administer justice. By me princes are exalted, and sovereigns rule the earth" (Prov 8:15). Finally, "Be subject to all the exalted authorities, for there is no authority except from God, and those which exist have been established by God (Rom 13:1).

The second argument comes by way of explaining the need and purpose of governance. "In Irenaeus' view, humanity has departed from God and has reached the apex of savagery. In response to this savagery, God imposed upon humans the fear of humanity because they did not recognize the fear of God."[6] This, moreover, allows for some degree of justice and forbearance in human society.

Consequently, "the State exists as God's creation for the purpose of ordering justice by penalizing injustice. This justice, however, can only be an external justice of outward appearance. The foundational cause of injustice and evil, the failure of humanity to fear God, allows for secret, hidden, internal sins."[7] Humanity is more disposed to perform like Cain than Abel, except for the restraints imposed by governance.

Those in authority will also have to give an account of their service. If they render justice faithfully, they will be commended. However, if they

---

6. Bingham, *God and Caesar*, 30.
7. Ibid.

subvert justice, they will perish. A person is expected to be faithful in his or her calling.

Irenaeus also asserts that God has instituted governance in a manner that fits those to be governed and the circumstances of the time. This results in a calculated diversity. Qualifications aside, the populace gets what it deserves.

He subsequently sets forth seven principles regarding the posturing of the state and church. First, human government exists at God's bequest. Then, by implication, it is good. The failure of governance can then be characterized as good having gone wrong. Conversely, governance is decidedly not the invention of Satan—to be resisted by pious resolve.

Second, Christians are obligated to pay taxes in support of legitimate activities associated with governance. Then, again by implication, to render other services associated with civil responsibility. If an exception, this ought not to be the rule.

Third, governance exists as a concession to humanity's refusal to fear God. Lacking a fear of the Almighty, they must contend with the authorities. In this regard, "For rulers hold no terror for those who do right, but for those who do wrong. Do you want to be free from fear of the one in authority? Then do what is right and he will commend you. For he is God's servant to do you good" (Rom 13:3–4).

Fourth, governance exists for a beneficial purpose by way of furthering justice. While not limited to distributive justice, it is especially striking in this regard. In particular, it helps refine the obligations of the populace for the common good. It, in addition, encourages compliance and discourages deviation.

Fifth, the efforts of governance in furthering peace and extending justice are consistent with God's benevolent design. Allowing for their manifest imperfection, they amount to approximate means. As such, they are along the line of transitory accommodations.

Sixth, governance may be for the better or worse. In this regard, the authorities and populace are inexorably linked. One is able to bring out the better or the worse in the other, and both are impacted by the corporate endeavor.

Seventh, governance does not supplant God's sovereign design for universal justice. Accordingly, "Righteousness exalts a nation, but sin is a disgrace to any people" (Prov 14:34). God thus allows for no exceptions.

Michael Bauman provides the third essay, graphically associated with *the dangerous Samaritan*. We thought we were doing the right thing when we "passed laws to raise their wages and lower their rent; if we gave generously to help support mothers without husbands and children without fathers, we would aid the poor in their flight from poverty and alleviate much of their distress while they were still in it. We were wrong."[8]

Good intentions proved to be inadequate. First, we thought that if we passed laws mandating higher wages for the lowest paid workers, we could increase their income, and thereby help them escape from poverty. We forgot that the lowest paid workers were normally those with the least skill and experience, and least desirable. By artificially raising wages, we made them even less desirable.

Second, we thought that by legislating a reduction of cost for urban housing, we could make available more inexpensive housing. We forgot that the more appealing to the renter, the less so to the owner. As a result, landlords wisely decided to allocate their investments in other ways.

Third, we thought that by providing welfare for the mothers of illegitimate children, we could make life easier for them and their offspring. We overlooked the fact that this would actually encourage persons to perpetuate their reliance from one generation to the next. This resulted in what is described as *a welfare culture*.

Fourth, by distributing funds among the poor, we thought it would simply be a means of aiding and comforting the unfortunate. We failed to take into consideration that poverty itself might not be the problem, but only a symptom. In failing to speak to the deeper need, we thus compounded the problem.

Worthy of note, "Christian love operates upon the premise that the defeat of poverty is a joint effort, or common endeavor, between the haves and the have nots, not an unilateral thrust by the haves only. The recipients of Christian charity ought to be either diligent workers or else unable."[9] In other words, there is a hierarchy of needs that have to be addressed.

"We can help the poor," Bauman concludes, "but we must do so as good, rather than dangerous, Samaritans." Accordingly, our initial tasks require: (1) Put our programs in the hands of contributors, not recipients or bureaucrats. As for the former, these may be expected to make a genu-

---

8. Bauman, *God and Caesar*, 201.
9. Ibid., 211.

ine effort to alleviate the problem. As for the latter, they are disposed to compound it.

(2) Redefine poverty. Nearly 40 percent of those designated as *poor* own their own homes, with more living space than enjoyed by most middle-class Europeans. Nearly 70 percent of America's poor own at least one car. Instead, *poverty* ought to retain its earlier connotation: the lack of food, shelter, or clothing.

(3) Re-educate the politicians and the poor. Bring to their attention that welfare can prove addictive and debilitating. Nor is it a shame to be poor; the shame lies in being slothful. All of which recalls a young lady, who had received a free college education, and refused to accept employment she thought below the level of her training.

(4) No perfect solutions are possible. Poverty cannot be eradicated, only ameliorated. The bad news is that all our efforts will fall short, while the good news is that there is much of constructive nature that can be done to improve the situation. In brief, this calls for realism.

(5) The rule of doing to others as we would have them do to us is critical to any effective initiatives to alleviate the needs of the poverty stricken. One should not request special considerations, but settle for what is implied by *distributive justice*. This involves a cooperative endeavor, consideration for the integrity of others, and righteous resolve. It is only as we empathize with the needs and aspirations of others, whether haves or have nots, that we can hope to make good progress. Then, too, good Samaritans are in great demand.

9

Legal Justice

This is a true story. It seems that a conscientious police officer closed a bar room which had exceeded its curfew. The case was postponed until a judge who could be bribed was on duty. Whereupon, he reprimanded the officer and warned him under penalty of being sentenced for unlawful entry not to intervene in the future.

The public servant was crestfallen. He deliberated whether to resign, or tolerate the injustice that was inflicted by the magistrate. At last report, he was undecided.

The problems with our legal system are legion. Some years ago, I was discussing the heavy backlog of cases waiting to be heard with a lawyer from Hong Kong. "We used to have the same problem," he allowed. "But when we decided to fine persons who brought trivial or improper suits, the problem was largely eliminated." Instead, litigation is encouraged and rewarded, resulting in added expense for medical treatment—among other objectionable results.

Statistics are revealing. It is reported that more persons have lost their lives in connection with people driving under the influence of intoxicating drink than in all our national conflicts combined. Still, the courts seem either to lack the resolve or means to curtail this tragic onslaught.

We noted in an earlier connection the occasion when Solomon was called upon to adjudicate a matter concerning two prostitutes. "My Lord, this woman and I live in the same house," one of them allowed. "I had a baby while she was there with me. The third day after my child was born, this woman also had a baby. We were alone; there was no one in the house with us" (1 Kgs 3:17–18).

"During the night this woman's son died because she lay on him. So she got up in the middle of the night and took my son from my side while I your servant was asleep. She put him by her breast and put my dead son to my breast." The next morning, when she had arisen, she saw the deceased child. Looking more closely, she realized that it was not her son.

"No!" the other protested. "The living one is my son; the dead one is yours." They continued to argue between themselves.

"Bring me a sword," the ruler ordered his attendant. Thus provided with the means, he ordered the child cut in two, so that each woman would retain half.

"Please, my lord," the genuine mother pled, "give her the living baby! Don't kill him!"

"Neither I nor you shall have him," the other taunted her. "Cut him in two!"

Then Solomon identified the first woman as the true mother, and mandated that the child be delivered to her. Thus, his reputation for wisdom was greatly enhanced, and the cause of justice admirably served.

Several related observations would seem in order. First, legal justice allows for no exceptions. Otherwise, the prostitutes might well have been neglected—since their vocation was frowned upon.

Second, each is to be given a legitimate hearing. The decision must be rendered based on pertinent evidence. Then manifestly not to show preference for one person over another.

Finally, the decision should be such as would solicit social approval. All too often this is not the case. Consequently, mistrust and cynicism result. The situation is inclined to deteriorate.

"How long will you defend the unjust and show partiality to the wicked!" the oracle protests. "Defend the cause of the weak and fatherless; maintain the rights of the poor and oppressed" (Psa 82:2–3). "We now detect the irony that the judges have now become the judged. More specifically, the administration of justice—in God's view—includes rescuing and delivering *the weak* and *the poor*."[1] Since these are least likely to be given proper consideration.

How long alerts us to the fact that injustice persists. Not only in exceptional instances, but also as standard practice. Once set in place, it is exceedingly difficult to eliminate.

---

1. Broyles, *Psalms*, 336.

"Among the people are wicked men," the prophet protests. "Their evil deeds have no limit; they do not plead the case of the fatherless to win it, they do not defend the rights of the poor" (Jer 5:26, 28). "The rich still oppress the poor in Judah, and it is impossible for a man to obtain justice in the courts. This was serious, since the Mosaic law had strong humanitarian overtones which required the Israelites to look to the welfare of the needy and underprivileged."[2]

The wicked men resemble social parasites. They seek by every means to accumulate wealth and privilege. In the process, they subvert legal justice. "Shall I not punish them for this?" the Lord rhetorically inquires. Indeed!

We next explore the establishment of Gentile courts in Jewish tradition, as a case study in legal justice. This injunction was said to have derived from God's covenant with Noah, as patriarch of the nations. Now when the waters had receded, Noah built an altar to the Lord, and sacrificed on it. This pleased the Lord, who pledged: "Never again will I curse the ground because of man, even though every inclination of his heart is evil from childhood. And never again will I destroy all living creatures, as I have done" (Gen 8:21).

Then God blessed the patriarch and his sons: "Be fruitful and increase in number and fill the earth." In keeping with this benediction, they were to partake of the produce of the earth—with the exception of eating meat with its *lifeblood still in it.*

Moreover, "Whoever sheds the blood of man, by man shall his blood be shed; for in the image of God has God made man" (9:6). The seriousness of the offence is attested to by that fact of humans being created in God's image. In this regard, "Judaism is like a three-legged stool. Upholding it are three kinds of sacredness: sacred space, sacred time, and sacred community."[3]

Then God said, "This is the sign of my covenant that I am making between me and you and every living creature with you, a covenant for all generations to come. I have set my rainbow in the clouds, and it will be the sign of the covenant between me and the earth." In this regard, the rainbow resembles a bow held over one's head as a sign of peace.

---

2. Harrison, *op. cit.*, 78–79.
3. Robinson,, *op. cit.*, 195.

Now the rabbis reasoned that God's covenant with Noah was in large measure an affirmation of that with Adam. In particular, it contained seven laws pertaining to idolatry, blasphemy, murder, theft, sexual relationships, eating the flesh of a living creature, and courts of law. It is the last of these on which we will focus our attention, as a means of insuring legal justice.

"In effect, the commandment to establish courts of law is a prohibition against failing to established (them), because failure to establish appropriate courts inhibits the performance of justice throughout the nations."[4] Otherwise, the social structure becomes chaotic. Then, too, the strong are tempted to prey on the weak.

Allowing for this distinction, the failure to establish courts of law results in a sin of omission. This, in turn, implies a deliberate choice. One that rejects God's righteous counsel.

The rabbis comment first in one connection and then another. Qualifications aside, one must accept the legal decision of the court. In doing so, he or she repudiates what might be called *vigilante justice*—whereby individuals or groups assume prerogatives to which they are not entitled.

Of course, persons are called upon to actively oppose such abhorrent practice as the Holocaust. The complicity of the courts in this matter was clearly in violation of the stipulations meant to guide the righteous Gentile. Most decisions are less obvious, and require earnest discernment.

The rabbis have debated at length the correlation between the Mosaic legislation and that recognized by the Gentile courts. As for the former, it goes into much greater detail. As for the latter, it is confined to the seven topics. Still, according to some Jewish commentary, these cover much the same area.

Then where there appears to be some deviation, which code is to take preference? The generally accepted opinion is that the person is bound by the particular Gentile code, assuming it is in keeping with the provisions of the covenant with Noah. This would allow creative diversity along with continuity.

"Arbitration and mediation or any other means of finding an amicable settlement or compromise, whereby avoiding a court trial, is desirable,

---

4. Clorfene and Rogalsky, *The Path of the Righteous Gentile*, 101–102.

and more than that, it is a commandment to seek compromise."[5] Here the term *compromise* is not used in its pejorative sense, implying tolerance of what is unacceptable. Instead, it is said that *compromise* in the sense of accommodating to the integrity of others is a necessary ingredient in any public forum.

In this connection, Jesus enjoined: "If your brother sins against you, go and show him his fault, just the two of you. If he listens to you, you have won your brother over. But if he will not listen, take one or two others along, so that every matter may be established by the testimony of two or three witnesses" (Matt 18:15–16). If he refuses to hear them, report it to the church. Then if he refuses to listen to the church, treat him as an unbeliever. An amicable settlement at the outset is certainly to be preferred to a long, drawn-out procedure—with uncertain results.

Circumstantial evidence was deemed admissible. It plays a more prominent role in judicial proceedings than we may realize. This was brought to my attention recently by a person who had for some years been involved in investigation. He observed that eyewitness reports were not very dependable, so that circumstantial evidence was as a rule required building a credible case.

He also indicated that no two cases were precisely the same. One had to work with what was available, and watch for the convergence of evidence. This characteristically called for a prolonged investigation, following up leads—most of which proved to be of little consequence.

The rabbis also insisted that it is unacceptable to disregard the taking of a person's life. Such as when someone reasons that capital punishment simply compounds the problem. Or to excuse the murderer on the ground that he or she was simply the product of society, and bears no personal responsibility in the matter.

This reasoning extends to the pointless delay of execution. Although this is thought to lessen its deterrent feature, it is a much debated issue. Then, too, it is claimed that the delay amounts to inhumane treatment. In any case, it contributes to the drain on public resources.

Similarly, the court must not excuse the poverty stricken person on the grounds that he or she should be given special consideration. This is not the place to address social inequalities. In proverbial terms, "Two wrongs do not make a right."

---

5. Ibid., 102.

The principle can be readily extended to embrace any person who claims special privilege. Such as the politician who argued that his offense should be overlooked, given all the good he had accomplished. He apparently felt this gave him permission to violate the law as a means of self-indulgence.

"If two litigants appear in court, and one is a righteous person while the other is a wicked person, the judge should not presume that the wicked person will not tell the truth, nor presume that he will not change his ways, and therefore the judgment would go against him."[6] This would be to prejudge the matter.

Conversely, the magistrate should not assume that the righteous person will necessarily be honest. His resolve may waver in this instance. Furthermore, there may be external pressures that cause him to misrepresent matters. While one's reputation may be worthy of the benefit of a doubt, it should not contravene evidence.

The rabbis seem determined to leave no stone unturned. A magistrate must not delay the trial, causing the litigants to suffer. He may be tempted to do so, as a means of emphasizing his own importance. Such falls short of righteous judgment.

It follows that lawyers must not be allowed to extend proceedings to increase their fees. This practice is calculated to pervert justice. Also, causing the populace to lose confidence in its judicial system.

Magistrates who judge haughtily, without sensing the awesome responsibility of their office, do so at great personal risk. In doing so, they show a disregard both for God and their fellow man. Neither is to be taken lightly.

This caution extends to those who act hastily and without due deliberation. These appear not to realize the gravity of the situation. They are inclined to approach their duties in a perfunctory fashion. They also fail to grasp the fact that in the manner they have judged, they will be judged (cf. Matt 7:2).

Each case must be judged on its own merits. There is no legitimate means of circumventing the sometimes arduous task of realizing legal justice. Every instance requires a fresh approach.

However, this does not preclude the use of legal precedence. Since this provides helpful guidelines for considered action. Accordingly, one

---

6. Ibid., 103.

can profitably draw upon a rich legal legacy to adjudicate. properly This is in keeping with the admonition to seek out the counsel of others (cf. Prov 11:14).

A magistrate must also treat the litigants similarly. In this connection, he should not allow one to speak at length, while limiting the other. Nor should he speak kindly to one, while gruffly to the other.

It is strictly forbidden to offer a bribe. This is an offense whether received or not. "Do not take away my soul along with sinners," the psalmist pleads, "my life with bloodthirsty men, in whose hands are wicked schemes, whose right hands are full of bribes" (26:9–10).

It is also not allowed to accept a bribe. "Do not accept a bribe, for a bribe blinds those who see and twists the words of the righteous" (Exod 23:8). As for clarification, "Bribes include any income which is acquired by government officials and judges through illegal means. They are generally received in support of a legal claim and are designed to influence the decision on that claim."[7] As such, they constitute a perversion of justice.

We next turn our attention briefly to the *Bet Din*/Jewish ecclesiastical court. While the Gentile courts were not required to follow their rules, they were encouraged to familiarize themselves with them. We will touch on several representative examples.

The litigants may either sit or stand, but it is not proper for one to sit and the other stand. However, when the magistrate's judgment is read, both should stand. Witnesses for either should stand during testimony.

Two principles are involved. First, the litigants are to be treated in the same manner. In particular, a more prestigious person should not be given special consideration. Second, one should stand out of respect for the judicial proceedings. It constitutes a solemn occasion.

If there are numerous cases pending, the case of an orphan should precede that of a widow, the widow that of a Torah scholar, the scholar that of an unlearned man, a woman that of a man—*because a woman's embarrassment is greater.*

The prime concern is to accommodate those who are less able to sustain the rigors of a court appearance. While the Torah scholar may be an exception, it perhaps assumes that he is advanced in age. In any case, he would be deserving of deference.

---

7. Walton and Matthews, *op. cit.*, 118.

The magistrate is forbidden to hear the plea of one of the litigants, while the other is not present. Moreover, the litigants are to be advised of this ruling. Should this rule be violated, the sentence will be overthrown.

The integrity of the court thus depends on the involvement of the magistrate and both litigants. In a larger sense, a fourth—God. The judiciary lacks credibility without recognition of its divine mandate.

The judge may not hear the testimony through a translator. The margin of error is too great. In proverbial terms, "One should say what he or she means, and means what he or she says."

This prohibition extends to the sentencing. It is critical that the litigants understand why the judge decided in favor of one and not the other, what penalty is anticipated, and what means there are (if any) for redress. It must also be borne in mind that since the litigants are under duress, they may be distracted.

In conclusion, every judge should possess the following attributes:

Wisdom

Humility

Fear of Heaven

Fear of sin

Contempt for money

Love of truth

Beloved by his fellow man

A good reputation[8]

If a magistrate cannot be found who qualifies in all these regards, one should strive to find someone who meets as many of the requirements as possible. In this and other ways, legal justice is admirably served.

---

8. Clorfene and Rogalsky, *op. cit.*, 108.

10

RETRIBUTIVE JUSTICE

RETRIBUTIVE JUSTICE SERVES AS AN EXTENSION OF THE PREVIOUS TOPIC. In particular, it concerns the assessment of punishment for criminal behavior. As such, it touches on several related areas—such as blood vengeance and cities of refuge.

The notion of *recompense* plays a critical role in retributive justice. This, in turn, draws from the persuasion that a person may expect to reap what he or she sows. The metaphor appears in various contexts. For instance, Jesus told a parable concerning a man who sowed good seed, in anticipation of a commensurate harvest. However, while everyone was sleeping, his enemy came and sowed weeds among the wheat. Then when the wheat sprouted, the weeds also appeared. "Sir," his servants inquired, "didn't you sow good seed in your field? Where then did the weeds come from?" (Matt 13:27).

"An enemy did this," he replied.

"Do you want us to go and pull them out?" his servants inquired further.

"No," he responded, "because while you are pulling the weeds, you may root up the wheat with them. Let both grow together until the harvest. At that time I will tell the harvesters: First collect the weeds and tie them in bundles to be burned; then gather the wheat and bring it into my barn."

The parable warns against the temptation of being unduly rigorous in disciplining errant members of the fellowship. As mentioned in an earlier context, the *lex talionis* serves a similar purpose. In cases of serious injury, "you are to take life for life, eye for eye, tooth for tooth, hand for hand, foot for foot, burn for burn, would for wound, bruise for bruise" (Exod 21:23–25). Nothing more, since this puts a strict limitation on what can be enacted by way of recompense.

Nor necessarily to this extent, should there be extenuating circumstances. In this regard, there were cities of refuge provided for those who had inadvertently killed another. Accordingly, "These six cities will be a place of refuge for Israelites, aliens and any other people living among them, so that anyone who has killed another accidently can live there" (Num 35:15).

In particular, this would discourage the practice of blood vengeance. The kinship group retaliated for the death of one of its members by this means. "Should the person leave the city of refuge at any time, *the avenger of blood may kill the accused*. If the accused stays *in the city of refuge until the death of the high priest*, then the person is free to return home."[1]

Now Jesus took issue with the application of recompense in private matters. "You have heard that it was said," he allowed, 'Eye for eye, and tooth for tooth.' But I tell you, Do not resist an evil person. If anyone smites you on the right check, turn to him the other also" (Matt 5:38–39). In context of the culture, he likely had in mind being struck by the back of the hand, as a demeaning insult—rather than with intent to injure the person. Even so, one should make a practice of returning good for evil.

Defaming the Almighty could invoke the death penalty. As an example, a certain Israelite cursed the name of God. Whereupon, he was put in custody, and brought before Moses. Then the Lord instructed him, "Take the blasphemer outside the camp. All those who heard him are to lay their hands on his head, and the entire assembly is to stone him" (Lev 24:14).

The execution occurred outside the camp, so that the ritual purification of the tabernacle and congregation would not be violated. Those who had heard the incriminating words were to attest to this by placing their hands on the prisoner's head. The *entire assembly* was to express its concurrence by participation.

The Sabbath observance was also to be taken seriously. "Observe the Sabbath, because it is holy to you," the people are enjoined. "Anyone who desecrates it must be put to death" (Exod 31:14). This has been described

---

1. Bellinger, *op. cit.*, 316.

as *desert law*, reflecting the precarious nature of their existence as a people group.

In terms more congenial, "It often needs to be pointed out that all the Sabbat laws are suspended in life-threatening situations. We are duly obliged to 'violate' the Sabbat to help someone who is dangerously ill. Also, we may not be 'overly pious' and refuse to accept help that involves a violation of the law."[2]

As touched on earlier, the wanton taking of a human life was strictly forbidden—under penalty of death. This pertained not only to the Israelites, but those living in their midst. Both alike were created in God's image and thus deserving of protection under the law.

Even so, the greatest of care had to be exercised to see that the charge was legitimate. Accordingly, "On the testimony of two or three witnesses a man shall be put to death, but no one shall be put to death on the testimony of only one witness" (Deut 17:6). This provides the means for purging *the evil from among you*.

Qualifications aside, one's culpability extends to the injuries inflicted by his animals. In this connection, "If a bull gores a man or a woman to death, the bull must be stoned to death. But the owner of the bull will not be held responsible. If, however, the bull has had the habit of goring and the owner has been warned but has not kept it penned up and it kills a man or woman, the owner also must be put to death" (Exod 21:28–29). Then should the bull gore a slave, the owner must pay thirty shekels of silver to the master of the slave, and the bull put to death. Worthy of note, the idea of *reparation* surfaces here and elsewhere as an additional concern in retributive justice. Suppose a person uncovers or digs a pit, and fails to cover it. Whereupon, an ox or donkey fall into it. In this instance, the owner shall pay for the loss— since he was manifestly negligent. He, however, retains the carcass.

The protection of property was a prime concern. "If a man's bull injures the bull of another and it dies, they are to sell the live one and divide both the money and the dead animal equally" (v. 35). If, on the other hand, it was known that the bull had the habit of goring, yet the owner failed to keep him penned up, he must reimburse for the loss and may keep the dead animal.

---

2. Eckstein, *How Firm a Foundation*, 68.

"If a man steals an ox or a sheep and slaughters it or sells it, he must pay back five head of cattle for the ox and four sheep for the sheep (22:1). "There is a heavier fine for this, since such action presumably shows deliberate intent to steal. Reparation for an ox is fivefold (as against fourfold for a sheep), since a trained ox is not only more valuable, but harder to replace."[3]

If a thief is caught breaking in during the night, and is injured so that he dies, the defender is guiltless. However, should it happen after sunrise, he is culpable. It goes without saying that the thief is obligated to make restitution, but should he be without the means to do so, he can be sold into slavery. This, in turn, provides a ready means for reparation.

If a person allows his livestock to graze on the land of another, he must make restitution. This must consist of *the best* he has to offer in return. It is not meant that he will simply break even.

Cattle-rustling and attacks by wild beasts were common threats to the society. If it could be demonstrated under oath, or by the mutilated carcasses of the animals, the person who was charged with caring for the animals would not be obligated for reparation. Otherwise, it was assumed that he was an accomplice.

Social relations were also a critical concern. "If a man seduces a virgin, who is not pledged to be married and sleeps with her, he must pay the bride price, and she shall be his wife. If her father absolutely refuses to give her to him, he must still pay the bride-price for virgins" (22:16–17). Qualifications aside, this was viewed as theft. Incidentally, demeaning one's reputation was perceived in similar manner.

The bride price is still invoked in many parts of the world today. It brings to mind an instance where the young man hoped to marry a girl from a more affluent family. Since her father had passed away, it was for her elder brother to negotiate the bride price. He set an exceptionally high amount, hoping to dissuade the couple. Instead, the fellow's extended family raised the required sum, and the couple happily married.

A sorceress was to be put to death. In more detail, "Let no one be found among you who sacrifices his son or daughter to the fire, who practices divination or sorcery, interprets omens, engages in witchcraft, or casts spells, or who is a medium or spiritist or who consults the dead"

---

3. Cole, *Exodus*, 171.

(Deut 18:10–11). These alike were *detestable* to the Lord, since they demonstrate a lack of confidence in the Mosaic tradition.

In this connection, "It was certainly safer to sacrifice a newborn than perform an abortion. For this reason, this author believes that the Old Testament is concerned with the practice of infant sacrifice, which might be considered the Canaanite counterpart to abortion."[4] If not abortion as such, then what is sometimes designated as *abortion for convenience*.

Those who treat their parents with contempt were liable for the death penalty (cf. Lev 20:9). This stands in contrast to the injunction that we honor our parents. The rabbis concluded that this involved relying on their counsel, respecting their wishes, caring for their needs, and remembering them in appropriate ways after their demise. This constituted the bedrock of society.

Those guilty of adultery were also subject to the death penalty. This was but one of the sexually impermissible practices such as incest, marriage within the immediate family, homosexuality, bestiality, and divorce. The norm was established early on: "For this reason a man will leave his father and mother and be united to his wife, and they will become one flesh" (Gen 2:24). The declaration that *they will become one flesh* relates primarily to the unique spiritual and social bond of the couple. It takes on the form of a covenant arrangement.

The extended family was more prominent in those days than currently. Arranged marriages were customary, and thought preferable. In addition, the marriage provided an alliance between the two families. Divorce was much more difficult to obtain, because of invested social interests.

Lacking an effective means of retributive justice, society unravels. This is graphically illustrated by an episode from the turbulent time of the judges. It is pointedly mentioned at the outset that in "those days Israel had no king" (Judg 19:1). In greater detail, "In those days Israel had no king; everyone did as he saw fit" (17:6). Anarchy reigned!

Now a Levite who lived in a remote areas in the hill country of Ephraim took a concubine from Bethlehem of Judah. "The status of the woman here is not the same as the 'concubine' who was a minor wife in a family system which allowed for both wives and concubines. In the absence of any mention of other wives, the term 'husband,' 'master,' 'father-

---

4. Hoffmeier, *Abortion*, 53.

in-law,' and 'son-in-law,' indicate that this woman is not one among many wives."[5]

She, however, was unfaithful to him. She left him because of some unnamed grievance, and returned to her parental home. There eventually developed in Israel two schools of thought concerning divorce. Shammai, the more rigorous of the two, insisted that divorce be permitted only when the partner was sexually promiscuous. Hillel, on the other hand, allowed divorce for relatively trivial reasons. For instance, it was said that divorce was permissible if one's wife burnt his breakfast.

When four months had passed, the Levite set out to recover his spouse. We are not told the reason for his delay. While his father-in-law welcomed him, nothing is said of his spouse. Accordingly, his father-in-law prevailed on him to stay three days—while enjoying his hospitality.

When the Levite proposed leaving, his father-in-law persuaded him to extend his visit. This occurred several times. As for apt commentary, "Hospitality was and still is a most important cultural value, and any deficiency in fulfilling one's obligations was/is looked upon as greatly shameful, even sinful. Thus what might be interpreted as the author's needlessly dragging out the story with endless repetitions and detail would have been in biblical culture a key element."[6].

Now when they drew near to Jebus/Jerusalem, the Levite's servant urged: "Come, let's stop at this city of the Jebusites, and spend the night." Incidentally, this was only five miles removed from their point of departure.

"No," the Levite replied. "We won't go into an alien city, whose people are not Israelites. We will go on to Gibeah." Since foreigners were not governed by covenant teaching, he supposed that they could not be trusted. He failed to take into consideration that the Israelites might be even less trustworthy.

They subsequently made their way to Gibeah, where they sat down in the city square. No one offered them hospitality, indicating a thorough disregard of social amenities. That evening an elderly man from the hill country of Ephraim returned from the fields. When he saw the neglected travelers, he extended hospitality to them.

---

5. Hamlin, *op. cit.*, 161–162.
6. Harris, Brown, and Moore, *Joshua, Judges, Ruth*, 271.

While they were enjoying themselves, some *wicked men* of the city surrounded the house. Pounding on the door, they demanded of the host: "Bring out the man who came to your house so we can have sex with him." This was a dual offense: gang rape in violation of the code of hospitality.

At this, the host attempted to dissuade them. "No, my friends" he protested, "don't be so vile. Since this man is my guest, do not do this disgraceful thing. Look here is my virgin daughter, and his concubine. I will bring them out to you now, and you can use them and do to them whatever you wish." He apparently thought this was the lesser of two evils, and the only option available to him. Of course, he may have hoped they would have reconsidered.

In any case, the host surrendered the Levite's concubine to them, and they abused her throughout the night. Then toward dawn, the woman made her way back to where her husband was staying, and collapsed at the door. When he opened the door, meaning to continue his journey, there lay his concubine. "Get up," he urged her, "let's go." When she failed to answer, he took his dead companion with him.

It is hard to imagine that retributive justice was so lacking that no effort was made to punish the perpetrators of this crime. The populace seemed quite indifferent. The wicked men are left to repeat their offense.

When the Levite reached his home, he cut up his concubine into twelve parts, and sent them to the tribes of Israel. Everyone who saw this graphic reminder observed: "Such a thing has never been seen or done, not since the day the Israelites came up out of Egypt." Then the Israelites demanded an accounting of what had happened.

Whereupon, they demanded that the Benjamites surrender the *wicked men* of Gibeah so that they might be executed. Retributive justice would finally have its day. Incidentally, the principle is one well attested in traditional cultures up to the present.

This recalls an incident reported by one of my West African students. It seems that his elder brother abused his wife, requiring that he be punished. The male members of the extended family gathered, and proceeded to beat the abusive husband. My student took part in the proceedings. In conclusion, he observed: "My brother is not likely to repeat his offense." More to the point, had the family failed to take action, the tribal officials would have felt obligated to take action.

When the Benjamites refused to turn over the *wicked men*, the Israelites slaughtered them in great numbers. Thus, belated justice was thought vindicated. However, failure to take earlier action had resulted in severe repercussions.

There is a third ingredient in retributive justice that should be identified in closing: namely, the prospect of *rehabilitation* (along with *recompense* and *reparation*). Now while the story of Jesus and the adulterous woman is not contained in our best manuscripts, it serves to illustrate the point. Certain of the scribes and Pharisees brought him an allegedly adulterous woman.

"Teacher," they observed—as noted in an earlier context, "this woman was caught in the act of adultery. In the Law Moses commanded us to stone such women. Now what do you say?" (John 8:5). "What they wanted to do was to put Jesus in a dilemma from which he could not escape. If he said to stone her he would violate the Roman law in pronouncing a death sentence without Roman authority. If he said to free her it would appear that he was soft on or ignoring the Monica Law."[7]

Then, too, if she had been caught in adultery, what became of her partner? He was no less implicated. Jesus bent down, and began writing in the sand. When they kept pressing him, he straightened up and said to them: "If any one of you is without sin, let him be the first to throw a stone at her." Then he bent down, and continued writing.

At this her accusers began to take their leave, beginning with the eldest ones—leaving Jesus alone with the adulteress. "Woman," Jesus inquired, "where are they? Has no one condemned you?"

"No one, sir," she replied.

"Then neither do I condemn you," Jesus responded. "Go now and leave your life of sin." In this manner, rehabilitation claims a legitimate role in retributive justice.

---

7. Carter, *John*, 68.

11

Justice and Poverty

Justice accommodates numerous other nuances. We have touched on *poverty* in association with justice several times, most notably concerning liberation theology, but now we will take a more deliberate approach. Other topics will follow in more or less random fashion, concluding with *the legacy of justice*. We have thus reached a pivotal point in the text.

The term *poverty* reveals different connotations. In general, it is applied to those lacking adequate clothing, shelter, and/or sustenance. In a more arbitrary fashion, the poor may own their own home, an automobile, and manage reasonably well. In biblical tradition, it came to refer to persons who turned to God in time of need—regardless of financial solvency.

"There was a rich man who was dressed in purple and fine linen and lived in luxury every day," Jesus allowed. "At his gate was laid a beggar named Lazarus, covered with sores and longing to eat what fell from the rich man's table. Even the dogs came and licked his sores" (Luke 16:19–21).

We are thus introduced to two contrasting characters, who persist throughout. The one is exceedingly rich, and the other pathetically poor. They live as if in two different worlds, the one characterized by indulgence, and the other by unrelenting austerity. In a just society, the two would find a way of accommodation.

There were many poverty-stricken persons at the time. "A progressive *concentration of possessions* heightened the struggle over the distribution of wealth in the first century A.D. Herod had taken over a very great deal of land through confiscation. These possessions were later sold by the Romans. Only those in possession of some capital were in a position to buy."[1] And so it was that the rich got richer, and the poor got poorer.

Some disabling disease contributed to Lazarus' situation. This recalls an innovative beggar I encountered some years ago in Romania. He would show up from time to time with one alleged handicap and then another: dragging a limp leg behind him, his arm in a sling, or some other problem. As a result, his professed plight was not convincing.

Insofar as the giving of alms is thought obligatory, it encourages persons to abuse the system. In some instances, children are purposely crippled in order to provide income for the family. It is more common that persons simply attempt to make the most of an unfortunate situation.

"The time came when the beggar died and the angels carried him to Abraham's side." He had apparently made use of his undesirable condition to get his priorities in order. This, in turn, recalls Job's apt appraisal: "Naked I came from my mother's womb; and naked I will depart. The Lord gave and the Lord has taken away; may the name of the Lord be praised" (Job 1:21).

Not so the affluent man! When he died, he was in torment. Looking up, he saw Abraham at a distance, and called out to him: "Father Abraham, have pity on me and send Lazarus to dip the tip of his finger in water and cool my tongue, because I am in agony in this fire."

Jesus employed the imagery of the Valley of Hinnom to convey the notion of being cast into hell, for it provided the location for refuse to be discarded. So it was that after a long day in my office, I would from time to time descend into the region—to look for potshards. This left me with the lingering impression that hell accommodates that which no longer serves the purpose for which it was intended.

Along this line, C. S. Lewis characterized hell as the last place a loving God reserves for those who would accept nothing preferable. He also conceives of persons moving further and further away from one another, as a result of their alienation. Thus, a person who lived next door would now be a day's travel distant. He likewise imagines that some will continue to speculate whether such a place exists. In any case, we would assume that the language is meant to be metaphorical.

---

1. Theissen, *Sociology of Early Palestinian Christianity*, 41.

"Son," Abraham compassionately replied, "remember that in your lifetime you received your good things, while Lazarus received bad things, but now he is comfortable here and you are in agony. And beside this, between us and you a great chasm has been fixed, so that those who want to go from here to you cannot, nor can anyone come over from there to us."

"Once again Jesus' teaching strikes at the heart of the theological assumptions held by many of his contemporaries. Surely the rich man, they would reason, exemplified a man who was blessed of God while the poor man has only suffered what he deserved."[2]

In this regard, Jesus was approached by a young man who inquired: "Teacher, what good thing must I do to get eternal life?" (Matt. 19:16).

"Why do you ask me about what is good?" Jesus replied. "There is only One who is good. If you want to enter life, obey the commandments." The man perhaps hoped to distinguish between what was necessary and of less consequence. In any case, Jesus assured him that unqualified obedience was required.

"Which ones?" the man insisted.

Jesus elaborated: "Do not murder, do not commit adultery, do not steal, do not give false testimony, honor your father and mother, and love your neighbor as yourself."

"All these I have kept," the young man assured him. "What do I still lack?" "His uneasiness reveals an instinctive human awareness that legalism falls short of God's intention. That he had not, in fact, fulfilled the requirement to love his neighbor as himself is brought out in the account as told in the *Gospel According to the Hebrews*"—a second century expansion of the text.[3]

Jesus answered: "If you want to be perfect, go, sell your possessions and give to the poor, and you will have treasures in heaven. Then come, follow me." This was not understood to be a general requirement, as illustrated by the supportive communities among Jesus' followers. In greater detail, "The radical attitude of the wandering charismatics was possible only on the basis of the material support offered to them by the local communities.... The two social forms of the Jesus movement were both associated and distinguished by a graduated pattern of norms."[4]

2. Evans, *Luke*, 249.
3. Mounce, *Matthew*, 184.
4. Thiessen, *op.cit.*, 22–23.

A current example may be helpful. The man was highly successful in the business world. Upon returning to his unpretentious living quarters in the suburbs, he would call a city mission—to see if it had any pressing need. Then determining what was required, he would authorize the mission to draw on his bank account. Only then would he sit down with his wife to enjoy their evening meal. In this connection, he resembled those in the support communities that made it possible for the itinerant disciples to carry on their rigorous ministry.

When the young man heard Jesus' words, he *went away sad*—since he had great wealth. Whereupon, Jesus said to his disciples: "I tell you the truth, it is hard for a rich man to enter the kingdom of heaven. Again I tell you, it is easier for a camel to go through the eye of a needle than for a rich man to enter the kingdom of God." The camel was the largest animal readily observable, while the needle was the smallest opening in a familiar object. An elephant subsequently replaced the camel in the Talmud and Koran, further expanding on the contrast.

When the disciples heard this, they were astonished and inquired: "Who then can be saved?" The prospect appeared bleak indeed!

Jesus gazed at them, and replied: "With man this is impossible; but with God all things are possible." Not things that are contrary to fact, such as the old conundrum: "Can God create a rock too large for him to lift?" Or whether he would fail to act in accordance with his righteous nature. Instead, all things that are genuinely feasible.

In particular, it was axiomatic in Hebrew thought that God is the author of salvation. Man's efforts fall pitifully short, so that the *self-made man* is a figment of the imagination.

Peter answered him, "We have left everything to follow you! What then will there be for us?" He intended to point out that they had done all that the rich young man was reluctant to do. In that case, what is to be their recompense?

Jesus' response indicates that they will reign with him, as fellow servants. For true greatness consists of service. "And everyone who has left houses or children or fields for my sake will receive a hundred times as much and will inherit eternal life. But many who are first will be last, and many who are last will be first." In particular, they will participate in the extended family of believers, their stewardship increased immeasurably, and their life abundantly fulfilled. Thus, justice would admirably be served.

We fast-forward next to the 1980 Consultation on the Theology of Development, involving about forty expert participants. Two concerns appear especially pertinent. Initially, "We are deeply disturbed by the inability or unwillingness of the governments of the world to grapple with this injustice and tragedy—associated with dire poverty."[5] Also, "We are deeply disturbed by the extent of apathy within the Christian church in the face of widespread suffering and injustice in the world."

Accordingly, the participants pledge themselves to give more deliberate attention to the situation. In addition, "We resolve to place greater trust in God and greater trust in each other in order to build relationships which will encourage and strengthen us in our common task to relieve poverty and injustice." Their resolve falls pointedly short of employing coercive means.

This amounts to a *kingdom ethic*, which recognizes God's sovereign concern for all. This, moreover, willingly embraces the cost of discipleship. In this connection: "Such grace is costly because it calls us to follow, and it is grace because it calls us to follow *Jesus Christ*. It is costly because it costs a man his life, and it is grace because it gives man the only true life."[6]

Good intentions not uncommonly fail to take into consideration the realities of a situation. For instance, some years ago there were complaints concerning *chicken pastors* in West Africa. It seems that the missionary task force had drawn back from church planting, turning the task over to the native people—who were better suited to accomplish this purpose. This left the missionaries free to undertake more specialized ministry, such as theological education. This seemed largely successful, especially as trained nationals joined in the activity.

Not all efforts were as promising. Recognizing that the church was in need of financial support, persons were encouraged to raise chickens. While this in some measure did relieve the problem, certain pastors were criticized for spending more time with their chickens than their flocks. Hence, the designation *chicken pastors*.

One other illustration will perhaps suffice. "Western missionaries find it hard to avoid direct interaction with selected individuals and groups. When the missionaries return to their home land, those they have

---

5. Sider (ed.), *Evangelicals and Development*, 15.
6. Bonhoeffer, *The Cost of Discipleship*, 47.

Justice and Poverty 91

helped . . . are tempted to build little empires, as the missionaries still collect donations for them."[7].

The result is that a particular group of people is assisted, while others go without. Moreover, this creates ill feeling among the people—since the procedure is manifestly unjust. Whether in this connection or some other, one of the critical problems in seeking to meet the needs of people is the attrition of resources through dispersal.

A number of related observations draw our attention. First, the poverty-stricken are characteristically overlooked in a materialistic society. This is intrinsically unjust.

The point is that we are not strictly speaking an island unto ourselves, but part of the common whole. Thus, what we do or fail to do has a bearing on others. Not simply our contemporaries, but subsequent generations as well.

Second, the appeal for justice is in keeping with good stewardship. In this regard, God enjoined Adam: "Be fruitful and increase in number; fill the earth and subdue it" (Gen 1:2). In other words, employ its resources responsibility.

This is possible only as we respect the integrity of one another. Not simply the power brokers, but the marginalized as well. Not merely those who befriend us, but those who return evil for good.

Third, the productive persons in our society should play a prominent role in the decision making process. More than any other, they have an invested interest in wise investment. They are also more likely to invoke a work ethic.

While this is not meant to exclude others, it brings a needed realism to the enterprise. This results in setting reasonable goals and priorities. Moreover, it is a discipline relatively lacking in a bureaucratic alternative.

Fourth, there is a need to correct former mistakes, and engage in new developments. While change is not necessarily for the better, constructive change should be resolutely pursued. Consequently, justice appears more in dynamic than static terms.

So it was that Abraham left his extended family, friends, and familiar surroundings. Moreover, he did not know precisely what the new circumstances would involve. Convinced, nonetheless, that God would bless his endeavor. In proverbial terms, "Nothing ventured, nothing gained."

---

7. Mathews, *Evangelicals and Development*, 97.

Fifth, the more some things change, the more other things remain constant. For instance, it is always proper to honor one's parents. The rabbis reasoned that this was not conditioned on whether they had a good disposition. In fact, by honoring them, their disposition would likely improve.

We would conclude that precedent thus plays an important role in the quest for justice/alleviation of poverty. According to the sage, "Those who fail learn from history but relive its tragic mistakes." C. S. Lewis counseled that persons read one classic book from the past for every contemporary one. If for no other reason, this alerts us to the cultural idiosyncrasies that pass for truth.

Sixth, we ought to involve expertise whenever possible. In fact, most of what we embrace as truth is derived from others. This being the case, it is best to choose our mentors carefully. This is in keeping with the particular discipline implicated, so that one does not defer to a theologian in matters associated with the astronomer.

Nonetheless, "The fear of the Lord is the beginning of knowledge, but fools despise wisdom and discipline" (Prov 1:7). "Wisdom is practical, aimed at conduct, but one must know the teachings of the sage and be guided by *the fear of the Lord*. The obtuseness of fools spills over into their wicked behavior. Hence, the frequent opposition between the righteous (or the wise) and the wicked (or the fool) through the book."[8] Thus, God is depicted as the prime factor in life's equation.

Seventh, cultural sensitivity serves the pursuit of justice. In this connection, I recall reading of a tribe that was exceedingly tolerant of threatening behavior. It apparently had to do with the notion that the gods were implicated, and should not be offended.

Conversely, the people supposed that someone who persisted in smiling, the smile was insincere. Since obviously not all occasions lent themselves to this response. Accordingly, it occurred to me that a missionary convinced that an upbeat attitude was a good witness might be sending the wrong message.

Eighth, since Jesus insisted that his kingdom was not of this world, one would suppose the ideal of justice would not be altogether realized in this life. This serves to warn us concerning utopian philosophies, which

---

8. Murphy and Huwiler, *op. cit.*, 18.

promise more than they can generate. Neither circumstances nor human nature would concur in this regard.

This is not to condone a fatalistic attitude that concludes nothing can be done to better the world in which we live. As sometimes expressed, expect great things from God. Moreover, attempt great things in his name.

Ninth, time and eternity are on the same wave-length. What is good for one is good for the other. Conversely, that which ignores one or the other is counterproductive.

Hence, the righteous person should be engaged in worthwhile enterprise. This is with the conviction that one with God can make a significant difference, as with Abel, Enoch, Noah, Abraham, and a host of others. For instance, "By faith Moses' parents hid him for three months after he was born, because they saw he was no ordinary child, and they were not afraid of the king's edict" (Heb 11:23).

Tenth, the concerns for justice/alleviation of poverty are preconditions for their realization. "Create in me a clean heart," the psalmist petitions, "and renew a steadfast spirit within me" (51:10). Do not let former attitudes prevail.

"Then there will be righteous sacrifice, whole burnt offerings to delight you." The congregation will celebrate their covenant relationship with the Almighty, and one another. Life will be exceedingly good.

"Who shall separate us from the love of Christ?" Paul rhetorically inquires. "Shall trouble or hardship or persecution or famine or nakedness or danger or sword? No, in all these things we are more than conquerors through him who loved us" (Rom 8:35, 37). *More than conquerors* leaves no room for doubt, given the abundance of God's enabling grace—whether in the present connection or some other.

12

Justice and Mercy

MERCY, LIKE GRACE, AMOUNTS TO UNMERITED FAVOR. It no more conflicts with justice than love negates holiness. In keeping with the previous topic, persons are particularly encouraged to be merciful to those in dire need. As an example, "blessed is he who is kind to the needy" (Prov 14:21).

William Newell was primarily known as a pastor and teacher, rather than a hymn writer. Yet while he was on the way to class, lyrics began to form in his mind. He made his way to an unoccupied classroom, and scribbled the words on the back of an envelope. He then handed them to Daniel Towner, who promptly set them to music. They serve as an appreciative commentary on divine mercy:

> O the love that drew salvation's plan!
> O the grace that bro't it down to man!
> O the mighty gulf that God did span
> On Calvary.
> Mercy there was great and grace was free,
> Pardon there was multiplied to me,
> There my burdened soul found liberty—
> At Calvary.

This, in turn, draws our attention to Jesus' account of the unmerciful servant. "Lord," Peter inquired of Jesus, "how many times shall I forgive my brother when he sins against me? Up to seven times?" (Matt 18:21).

Since the rabbis reasoned that one should be forgiven up to three times, Peter's inquiry appears generous. Then, again, he may have simply been asking if it depends on a given situation.

Jesus answered, "I tell you, not seven times, but seventy-seven times." In other words, one should not put any limitation on forgiveness. Providing, that is, the conditions for forgiveness are met. In particular, repentance, resolve, and restitution. Otherwise, the offer of forgiveness remains.

Jesus subsequently observed: "the kingdom of heaven is like a king who wanted to settle accounts with his servants. As he began the settlement, a man who owed him ten thousand talents was brought to him. Since he was not able to pay, the master ordered that he and his wife and his children and all that he had be sold to pay the debt."[1] "Although taxes were exorbitant in those days, especially for rural peasants, Josephus reports the annual tribute from Galilee and Perea under wealthy Herod to be only two hundred talents; it was thus inconceivable that one official could get so far in debt." It would therefore appear obvious that Jesus employed hyperbole.

The servant fell on his knees, imploring his master: "Be patient with me, and I will pay back everything." Accordingly, the master *took pity on him*, cancelled the debt, and allowed him to go free. He thus far exceeded the request of his servant.

However, when the servant left, he encountered a fellow servant who owed him a relatively modest amount. The latter fell on his knees, begging him: "Be patient with me, and I will pay you back." But he refused. Instead, he had the man thrown into prison until he could pay the debt. Someone in prison lacked the means to pay back the debt, unless friends came to his aid.

When the other servants heard what had transpired, they were incensed. Accordingly, they reported the matter to their master. He, in turn, summoned his vindictive servant. "You wicked servant," he remonstrated, "I cancelled all that debt of yours because you begged me to. Shouldn't you have had mercy on your fellow servant just as I had on you?" Whereupon, he "turned him over to the jailors to be tortured, until he should pay back all he owed." While Jewish law prohibited torture, it was common prac-

---

1. Keener, *op. cit.*, 95.

tice in Gentile circles, and not uncommon even in Jewish society. In this instance, he had alienated persons, and could expect no reprieve.

"This is how my heavenly Father will treat each of you unless you forgive your brother from your heart," Jesus solemnly concluded. "An unwillingness to extend mercy is proof that a person has never received mercy. God's forgiveness must of necessity create a forgiving spirit."[2] *From your heart* touches on one's sincerity.

Jesus dealt more succinctly with the topic on an earlier occasion. Upon seeing the crowds, he went upon on a mountainside, sat down—in preparation for teaching, and addressed his disciples. The disciples had until recently been indistinguishable from the multitude. Even now, their separate identity was not as clearly marked as would subsequently be the case. The great divide would widen into a chasm with eternity.

Jesus began by reciting eight beatitudes. While commentators disagree as to whether they focus on the present or future, both aspects may be in mind. Initially, he observes: "Blessed are the poor in spirit, for theirs is the kingdom of heaven" (Matt 5:1). As previously observed, this pertains to those who turn to God as a result of their realized need. To be *blessed* is to enjoy the Lord's favor, regardless of circumstances. More to the point, "Blessed are the merciful, for they will be shown mercy." This reverses the pattern observed above: not only is mercy indicative of having received mercy, but also reveals that we shall receive mercy. The disciple is thus portrayed as a work in progress.

This perhaps brought to mind a classic text, "For I desire mercy, not sacrifice; and acknowledgment of God rather than burnt offerings" (Hos 6:6). "No sacrifice, no ritual repentance can substitute for that intimate relation of cleaving to God. And of course what God desires, and not what human beings desire, finally determines the destiny of all people."[3]

In other words, the ultimate sacrifice is that of self. This embodies justice/mercy, along with other righteous attributes. Obedient trust is a requisite.

Since we considered Jesus' parable concerning the good Samaritan in another context, we need to go into detail at this juncture. Suffice to say, the Samaritan *took pity on* the victim (cf. Luke 10:33). This was in contrast to the priest and Levite, of whom better things were expected.

2. Mounce, *Matthew*, 178.
3. Achtemeier, *Minor Prophets I*, 51.

On another occasion, Jesus observed: "There was a man who had two sons. The younger one said to his father, 'Father, give me my share of the estate'" (Luke 15:11–12). Therefore, his father divided his property between his sons, the elder son getting a double portion. To ask for one's inheritance in advance was exceedingly uncommon. It amounted to treating one's parents as if they were already deceased.

Not long after, the prodigal liquidated his holdings, and set off for a distant country. This served to confirm the worst scenario. After he had squandered his inheritance *in wild living*, he hired himself out to a Gentile. The latter, in turn, put him to work feeding his pigs—a ceremonially unclean animal, indicative of the defilement of this individual.

He longed to satisfy his hunger with the pods the pigs were eating, while no one offered to assist him. Although the nature of the *pods* is uncertain, the thought of eating pigs' food would have been disgusting to Jesus' hearers. Consequently, this served to illustrate graphically the man's desperation.

When he *came to his senses*, he recalled how many of those hired by his father had food to spare. Whereupon, he determined to return, and ask his father for employment. He "returns simply out of hunger and belief that his father may feed him as a servant, not because he is genuinely sorry that he disgraced his father. Given the magnitude of his sin, Jewish hearers might regard his return an act of incredible presumption rather than humility."[4]

While he was still at a distance, his father saw him and was filled with compassion for his son. One gets the impression that he had been searching the horizon in hope that the prodigal would return. This would certainly be in keeping with his general demeanor. Whereupon, he ran to greet his son, then embraced and kissed him.

"Father," his son protested, "I have sinned against heaven and against you. I am no longer worthy to be called your son." Or enjoy the privileges associated with the relationship. *Against heaven* was a cautious way of referring to God, since persons were warned not to take his name in vain (cf. Exod 20:7).

"*Quick!*" his father instructed the servants. "Bring the best robe and put it on him. Put a ring on his finger and sandals on his feet. Bring the fattened calf and kill it. Let's have a feast and celebrate."

---

4. Keener, *op. cit.*, 78.

The *best robe* would likely belong to his father, and the ring bearing a family crest. These, along with sandals, combined to indicate that he was welcomed back into the family circle.

The *fattened calf* anticipates a gathering of people. As in the case of marriage, the birth of a child, or reaching maturity. In this instance, his father explained: "For this son of mine was dead and is alive again, he was lost and is found." So they began to celebrate.

Meanwhile, his elder brother was in the field. Had none thought to summon him? Perhaps they had come to take his labors for granted.

When he drew near to the house, he heard the sound of music and dancing. So he called one of the servants, to inquire as to what was going on. "Your brother has come," the latter replied, "And your father has killed the fattened calf because he has him back safe and sound." The elder brother was furious, and refused to join the festivities. Then, in subtle manner, we are alerted to the fact that he lacked mercy.

So his father went out, and pleaded with him. "Look!" his elder son exclaimed. "All these years I've been slaving for you and never disobey your orders. Yet you never gave me even a young goat so I could celebrate with my friends. But when this son of yours who has squandered your property with prostitutes comes home, you kill the fattened calf for him!"

The failure to address him as *father* or *sir* was a serious breach of custom. This was compounded by the subsequent charges made against him. In addition, *prostitution* was strictly prohibited. The implication is that his father had been negligent.

"My son," his father tried to reason with him, "you are always with me, and everything I have is yours. But we have to celebrate and be glad, because this brother of yours was dead and is alive again; he was lost and is found." He thus counters the expression *this son of yours* with *this brother of yours*. In proverbial terms, "blood is thicker than water."

As for apt commentary, "the rabbis attached no less value to repentance than Jesus. They, too, urged that God cared more for the repentant than for the just who had never yielded to sin. But to *seek out* the sinner, . . . in order to work his moral redemption, this was something new in the history of Israel."[5] In other words, to approach persons not as they were but as they might become was remarkably unique.

---

5. Montefiore, *Jesus*, 159.

We will allow the teacher a final word, "there is a time to mourn and a time to dance" (Eccles 3:4). This was manifestly of the latter variety. However, we are not told whether the elder brother reconsidered.

This next section deals with what might be described as *the way of mercy*. It implies a rigorous course that must be negotiated. There are also obstacles and distractions to be resolved. As implied earlier, it is not only compatible with justice, but a necessary component.

The initial aspect seems to lack a suitable designation. I eventually settled on the notion of *tolerance*, although this does not mean to imply passivity. As relates to the Almighty, he is everywhere present and everywhere active.

This, in turn, recalls the prime example of Hosea. "It all began with a marriage. But the marriage of Hosea and Gomer was no ordinary nuptial. Initiated by the word of God, it was permeated with the purposes of revelation."[6]

In particular, the Lord enjoined Hosea: "Go, take to yourself an adulterous wife and children of unfaithfulness, because the land is guilty of the vilest adultery in departing from the Lord" (Hos 1:2). His wife and children are thus illustrative of the degenerate situation that gripped the land.

Be forewarned, "I will make her (Gomer) like a desert, turn her into a parched land, and slay her with thirst" (2:3). Her indulgence will leave her empty. Then she will conclude, "I will go back to my husband as at first, for there I was better off than now."

Be encouraged, "I will betroth you to me forever; I will betroth you in righteousness and justice, in love and compassion" (2:19). *Righteousness and justice* are the first couplet mentioned. "*Righteousness* describes Yahweh's commitment to be all that his covenant role as Sovereign and Savior demands and to relate to her in strength, loyalty and uprightness. *Justice* centers on Yahweh's fairness in all his relationships to his people, as he honors their obedience and corrects their waywardness."[7]

Love and compassion (mercy) are the second pair. As for the former, "*Steadfast love* rings with the tone of covenant loyalty, describing both the attitude and the behavior of the Lord who made a plea to his people to full

---

6. Hubbard, *Hosea*, 19.
7. Ibid., 88.

freedom." As for the latter, "*Mercy* glows with tenderness and compassion, especially as it shows itself to the weak, the needy, the oppressed."

The second aspect concerns *forgiveness*. In this regard, Paul admonishes his readers: "Be kind and compassionate to one another, forgiving each other, just as in Christ God forgave you" (Eph 4:32). By way of contrast, "Get rid of all bitterness, rage and anger, brawling and slander, along with every form of malice."

Forgiveness implies the willingness to set aside former grievances. To forgive is the prerogative of the one who has been offended. Accordingly, it can not be merited.

Moreover, forgiveness can best be appreciated in context of God's lavish blessing. In this connection, "Praise the Lord, O my soul, and forget not all his benefits—who forgives all your sins and heals all your diseases, who redeems your life from the pit and crowns you with love and compassion, who satisfied your desires with good things so that your youth is renewed like the eagle's" (Psa 103:2–5).

All his benefits initially involves life. In Jewish tradition, life is essentially good, and meant to be cherished. The rabbis reasoned that enjoyment was enhanced on the Sabbath, as we reflect on God's goodness. Also, that life is good in its particulars. Such as good health, loving family, devoted friends, and favorable circumstances. No less than when God sustains us through some crisis.

More expressly with regard to forgiveness. There follows three extended allusions. Initially, he *heals all your diseases*. In rabbinic thought, God heals us of all our diseases but the last. He may employ different means.

Secondly, he *redeems you from the pit*. While *the pit* might have reference to any hole in the ground, it naturally brings to mind a cistern. It was dark, usually damp, rocky, and isolated. One would be tempted to despair.

Thirdly, he *crowns you with love and compassion* (mercy). These combine to express God's determination to do the best in, and make the best of any facet of the relationship. Therefore, that even seemingly inconsequential matters may result in manifold blessing.

Finally, he *satisfies your desires with good things*, so that *your youth is renewed like the eagle's*. As when the eagle seems to glide effortlessly through the sky, unencumbered by the concerns that plague mere mortals. Such is the legacy of forgiveness.

The final aspect pertains to *restoration*. In general, "Have mercy on me, O God, according to your unfailing love" (Psa 91:1). In particular, "Restore to me the joy of your salvation and grant me a willing spirit, to sustain me" (v. 12). Here restoration involves not only the renewal of the relationship, but a righteous resolve to enhance it.

The ascription alerts us to the fact that this psalm recalls the time when the prophet Nathan rebukes David for committing adultery with Uriah's wife Bathsheba. David then conspired to have Uriah killed. "There were two men in a certain town, the one rich and the other poor," Nathan allowed (2 Sam 12:1). The rich man had a very large number of sheep and cattle, but the impoverished man had only one little ewe lamb—that he greatly cherished. Now when the rich man was called upon to offer hospitality, instead of providing one of his own animals, he confiscated the solitary lamb of his neighbor.

David was furious. "As surely as the Lord lives, the man who did this deserves to die" he exclaimed. "He must pay for the lamb four times over, because he did such a thing and had no pity."

Then Nathan solemnly declared, "You are the man!" After that, he recalled how the Lord had richly blessed him in the past.

"I have sinned against the Lord," David contritely confessed. While his sin would have serious repercussions, he was restored to favor. In this connection, "As Solomon grew old, his wives turned his heart after other gods, and his heart was not fully devoted to the Lord, as the heart of David his father had been" (1 Kgs 11:4).

It can thus be seen that the path of mercy runs true to course, while exhibiting tolerance, forgiveness, and restoration. In can also be said that justice employs mercy to achieve its purpose. Especially is this the case when God is invoked, and persons are available to his leading. Accordingly, it bears repeating:

> Mercy there was great and grace was free,
> Pardon there was multiplied to me,
> There my burdened soul found liberty—
> At Calvary.

13

Justice and Freedom

This topic recalls what struck me as an amusing incident at the time. My mother had the habit of telling her offspring what she would prefer that they do, and then leaving the decision up to them. This was remarkably successful with my sisters, who would forgo their preference in order to please mother. However, my brother was of a more independent nature.

The detail is still fresh in my memory. In response to my brother's inquiry, mother stated her preference—leaving the matter up to him. "Do you really mean it?" he incredulously inquired.

"Yes," she responded, her voice seeming to waver. Whereupon, my brother bolted out the door, bent on pursuing his own interests. This was the last time we children were given this option. It remained to follow our mother's directive, or suffer the unenviable consequences.

It goes without saying that we exercise freedom within constraints. Now the Lord God planted a garden, and deposited man therein. It was an enviable situation, drawing upon the associated imagery. Man was instructed to care for the garden. In return, he could partake of its produce—with the exception of the tree of the knowledge of good and evil. Otherwise, he would perish.

Initially, we are alerted that there is fallout from our decisions. While some may enhance freedom, others are calculated to inhibit it. Consequently, much is at stake.

This, in turn, invites us to consider the nature of freedom. In context of the Genesis account, it would appear that it entails ready access to God and life together. Accordingly, license does not qualify as freedom.

Now when the humans chose to disregard God's prohibition, they were turned away from the idyllic garden setting, and required to wander about—managing as best they could. While they had hoped to improve on their condition, they had squandered a prized opportunity. In Jewish tradition, this was said to culminate with bondage in Egypt—designated as man's seventh falling away.

Conversely, it marked the occasion of a divine initiative. It would result in a covenant people, meant to serve as a light to the Gentiles. No one said that the task would be easy. Hardly had the Israelites escaped captivity when they began to complain. "It would have been better for us to serve the Egyptians than to die in the desert!" they protested (Exod 14:12).

When on the verge of entering the promised land, they had second thoughts. As a result, a generation perished in the wilderness. Even so, the wilderness was recalled in terms of their encounter with the Almighty. As a result, persons retired to the wilderness to enhance their spiritual life.

When at last they made their way into the promised land, they failed to drive out its inhabitants. These served to compromise their identity as a people set apart for God's purposes. In particular, they were called upon not only to intercede on their own behalf, but of others.

The time of the judges was chaotic, with persons doing whatever seemed right in their own eyes. Without regard for their covenant commitment or social amenities. There was no centralized authority in those days.

As noted early on, it was the inevitable task of the prophets to fine-tune the monarchy to it covenant ideals. In spite of their zealous effort, the Northern Kingdom succumbed to the Assyrians. The Southern Kingdom fared better, benefitting from periodic renewals. Even so, the Babylonian captivity ensued.

The prophets, who had diligently warned of the impending disaster, now cultivated a vibrant hope. For instance, "In the time of my favor I will answer you, and in the day of salvation I will help you" (Isa 49:8). The best was yet to come.

When the exiles were at last permitted to return, the situation was not as envisioned. Not only did the nations fail to assemble to honor the Lord, but also the inhabitants proved to be hostile. Still, the faithful viewed what was sometimes designated as *the second exodus* as a prelude to the Messianic Age.

The Messianic profile was nonetheless ambiguous. "On the one hand, it appeared as if God Himself would intervene; on the other, as if through a chosen agent. On the one hand, the Messiah appeared as a military figure; on the other, as a heavenly agent. On the one hand, he was represented as a royal heir to David's throne; on the other, as a suffering servant."[1] This led some, as those associated with the Dead Sea Scrolls, to project two Messiahs—one in the priestly cast and the other of royal lineage.

This brief sketch of salvation history serves two related purposes. First, each person is one of *many*. Justice/freedom must consequently be understood in a corporate setting. What others do or fail to do has long range implications.

As an example, some persons are born into poverty. One of my Nigerian students received his first pair of shoes when twelve years of age. Incredible as it may seem, he procured an earned doctorate, and enjoyed a fruitful ministry.

Second, each of us is *one* of many. Some enjoy better physical health than others do. Dispositions vary. We respond differently to similar situations. There are no carbon copies. Given such great diversity, we ought not to be inclined to judge the intentions of others.

One of our neighbors was a devout mother of a large family. It concerned her that the Scripture teaches that the godly will suffer, while she seemed not to qualify. It apparently did not occur to her that the provocation she experienced in raising her children might justify her inclusion. She appears to have considered it a privilege.

This, in turn, invites us to explore the exodus more in detail, as a prime example of justice/freedom. The Greek historian Herodotus graphically described Egypt as *the gift of the Nile*. A strong centralized government was thought necessary to utilize the waters of the Nile most efficiently. "People of different races moved into the Nile Valley long before the dawn of history. . . . Although theoretically all land belonged to

---

1. Inch, *Exhortations of Jesus According to Matthew* and *Up From the Depths*, 82.

the king, in practice the Egyptian treated their soil, cattle, and homes as private property, paying the required taxes to the government."².

Now Joseph was sold by his brothers into slavery. In retrospect, he would assure them: "You intended to harm me, but God intended it for good to accomplish what is now being done, the saving of many lives" (Gen. 50:20).

"Throughout the ordeal God had led him and protected him, elevating him to leadership in the Egyptian government at a crucial time, thereby enabling him to save their lives and those of numerous people throughout that region. This view of divine providence accords with the teaching of wisdom literature. Humans make plans, but God determines the outcome (Prov. 16:9: 19:21)."³

God thus preserves both justice and freedom, not one to the exclusion of the other.

"Then a new king, who did not know about Joseph, came to power in Egypt" (Exod 1:8). This likely indicated a change in dynasty. Such would invite a reconsideration of past policies, and the anticipation of a new agenda.

"Look," the ruler pointed out to the populace, "the Israelites have become much too numerous for us. Come, we must deal shrewdly with them or they will become even more numerous and, if war breaks out, will join our enemies, fight against us and leave the country." As for the latter, their economic viability would suffer.

Therefore, they determined *to oppress them with forced labor*. "Forced labor was an old principle in highly-centralized Egypt, as in all the ancient world: neither pyramids nor Nile canals would have been possible without it. *Task-masters* is a technical term, and would describe the hated Egyptian officials, under whom there were minor Israelite officials."⁴

"But the more they were oppressed, the more they multiplied and spread; so the Egyptians came to dread the Israelites and worked them ruthlessly." Pharaoh decreed: "Every boy that is born you must throw into the Nile, but let every girl live." It was envisaged that in this way the remaining Israelites would be assimilated.

---

2. Pfeiffer, *Old Testament History*, 130.
3. Hartley, *op. cit.*, 367.
4. Cole, *op. cit.*, 54.

This was no idle threat, although we do know how extensive the slaughter was. In any case, Moses' parents kept him hidden away as long as it seemed feasible. Then his mother placed the infant in a papyrus basket, and set it afloat among the reeds. She left his sister at a distance, to observe what would transpire.

When Pharaoh's daughter came to bathe, she saw the basket in which the infant had been placed, and took pity on him. This encouraged his sister to inquire whether to secure a Hebrew woman to nurse the child. Receiving an affirmative reply, she enlisted his mother. Later on, Moses was adopted into the royal household.

Having attained maturity, Moses went out to where *his own people* were involved in oppressive labor. When he saw an Egyptian beating one of them, he looked first in one direction and then another, lest he be observed. Then he killed the offender. When this became known, he fled to Midian—to escape the wrath of Pharaoh.

Sometime later, he was tending his father-in-law's flocks in the vicinity of Horeb—*the mountain of God*. It is uncertain whether this designation was derived from a religious association prior to the giving of the covenant or as a result. As a matter of record, it was customary to erect one sanctuary on the site of a previous one.

Moses then observed a burning bush that was not consumed. "Natural explanations for the burning bush have been plentiful, from bushes that exude flammable gas to those covered with brightly colored leaves or berries."[5] However, no explanation is given. It was, in any case, consistent with other theophanies (manifestations of God).

God subsequently reveals himself to Moses, along with his intent to free the Israelites from bondage. Moses was to be his instrument. "Who am I, that I should go to Pharaoh and bring the Israelites out of Egypt?" the patriarch protested.

"I will be with you," God assured him. This, in turn, recalls the saying: "One with God is in the majority." Accordingly, Moses acquiesced.

It came to pass that he informed Pharaoh: "The Lord, the God of the Hebrews, has sent me to say to you: "Let my people go, so that they may worship me in the desert"" (Exod 7:16). This was a means of serving justice, while requiring the willing cooperation of the populace.

---

5. Walton and Mathews, *op. cit.*, 87.

Now when the ruler refused, successive plagues ravaged the land. Some have observed that these served to demonstrate the impotency of select deities. This was certainly true insofar as the pantheon was unable to cope with the threat.

Others have pointed out that the first nine plagues could be the result of natural phenomena, such as the flooding of the Nile. However, this would still not account for the extent of the plagues, nor their fortuitous timing. Efforts to account for the tenth plague, concerning the death of the first-born, have not been convincing. It appears especially aimed at the ruler, and his oppression of God's first-born—Israel.

Now when Pharaoh relented, the Israelites took leave to observe a solemn convocation in the wilderness. When pursued, God delivered them. Destiny awaited their arrival at Sinai.

The Passover recalls this deliverance as the seminal event in Jewish history. From this "some of the most profound affirmations of the Jewish people were drawn. Most notable among these was that God is present in human lives, that he hears the cries of the suffering and tormented, and that he intervenes in history to redeem him from oppression."[6]

God is present in human lives. He is no less immanent than transcendent. As for the former, he is nearer than our next breath.

Where can I flee from your presence?" the psalmist rhetorically inquires. "If I go up to the heavens, you are there; if I make my bed in the depths, you are there. If I rise on the wings of the dawn, if I settle on the far side of the sea, even there your hand will guide me, your right hand will hold me fast" (Psa 139:7–10).

He hears the cries of the suffering and tormented. Not simply on some select occasion, but as a matter of course. Then in contrast to those who have ears for hearing but fail to do so (cf. Matt 13:13).

He appears especially solicitous of those in grievous need. As if to recognize the urgency of their situation. In this manner, he sets the example for others.

Then, too, *he intervenes in history to redeem him from oppression.* Most noteworthy at critical junctures; as with the exodus, the historic struggle of the prophets with Baalism, and during the times of Jesus and the apostles. As a result, all are beneficiaries.

---

6. Eckstein, *op. cit.*, 76.

"Into your hands I commit my spirit," the psalmist acknowledges; "redeem me, O Lord, the God of truth" (Psa 31:5). No less the God of justice, who sponsors the responsible use of our opportunities. Thus does the exodus narrative assure us.

We next look at justice/freedom in a contemporary setting. Stephen Monsma protests a mind-set that perceives religion "as having only a private, personal relevance and lacking a real social or political impact. In fact, it views religion, when wedded to issues of social and political import, as a divisive, intolerant, and dangerous force."[7] This stance is promoted with reference to Thomas Jefferson's misappropriated metaphor of a *high wall of separation*.

Conversely, the non-establishment and free exercise of religion stipulations in the Bill of Rights was meant to allow for a dynamic interaction that disallowed a state sponsored religion. Instead of a high wall of separation, it was more along the lines of *helping hands*.

In terms of public education, this implies an earnest appraisal of the religious factor in the cultural equation. This is most obvious in the realms of history and literature. As for the former, religion plays a prominent role not only in the founding of the country, but also in its subsequent development. Should our political agenda fail to accurately portray our past, we put at risk our future.

Then, too, literature contains an abundance of biblical allusions. Accordingly, we do ourselves a disservice by failing to understand their intent. This extends to the original, as well as its application.

The issue carries over into the natural sciences in a more subtle manner. Strictly speaking, science pertains to that which can be empirically verified. Anything beyond this juncture ought to be construed as philosophy. There are, for instance, a variety of theories set forth to explain the origin of the universe and the proliferation of life—none of which can be verified. Consequently, it would seem that if we were to set forth an evolutionary model, we ought to recognize first the religious variant, and then the preference for intelligent design.

Otherwise, we court a secular establishment—one that precludes religious options. In this regard, the eminent theologian Paul Tillich reminds us that whatever fulfills the role of religion, is in fact a religion. He then defines religion is terms of *ultimate concern*. This would suggest

---

7. Monsma, *Positive Neutrality*, 175.

that a secular monopoly in public affairs is in essence a violation of the non-establishment provision.

"Pluralism, in contrast, leads to a quite different perspective with which to approach church-state issues. This mind-set colors everything else, and thus is crucial in setting the context from which the more specific, concrete standard of positive neutrality emerges."[8] In particular, Monsma cites a *positive* outlook on the contributions of religion in American society, and a genuine commitment to the free exercise of religion.

This assumes a realistic appraisal, one that recognizes human endeavor characteristically falls short of its aspirations. Religious folk ought not to be singled out for their failures, but pitied—along with the rest. Jesus appropriately cautioned, "You hypocrite, first take the plank out of your own eye, and then you will see clearly to remove the speck from your brother's eye" (Matt. 7:5).

The free exercise of religion involves not only freedom for those of differing religious perspectives, but persons without a religious orientation. As implied above, these have something that substitutes for a religious faith—commonly along the line of humanism. Religious pluralism thus envisages a situation where persons of diverse persuasion can interact in a constructive manner.

This ideal is notably free of coercion. Either from those of religious persuasion, or otherwise. Since *coercion* is an indication of an establishment mentality. As when public school officials choose to disregard the religious sensitivities of the families they serve, thus failing to recognize the cooperative nature of our educational mandate.

The scope of Monsma's thinking can be seen in the fundamental roles he assigns to religion. Initially, "All faith communities and religious associations cultivate, nurture, and develop their core beliefs in the lives of their adherents The first role involves developing, shaping, interpreting, and affirming a religion's basic answers to ultimate questions."[9] The remaining roles concern cultivating ethical behavior, providing a wide variety of services to members and others in society, and participation in society's policy-making process. Religious associations such as the United States Catholic Conference, the Israeli-American Public Affairs Committee, and the Christian Legal Society serve as representative

---

8. Ibid.
9. Ibid., 161.

agents. Thus, the concern for justice/freedom continues to run its course in contemporary American society.

14

JUSTICE AND LIFE

THE CURRENT TOPIC RECALLS A STORY I CAME ACROSS SOME YEARS AGO. It seems that an Eskimo family was making its way across the frozen tundra, as night was approaching. The grandmother solemnly announced that her life was ebbing away, and that they should leave her by the campfire to succumb. Although her daughter attempted to convince her otherwise, it was to no avail. The aged grandparent reasoned, "The bear will eat me, and my grandson will eat the bear." Thus, life continues from one generation to the next.

I am also reminded of a memorable episode that took place during World War II. The Nazi regime had determined that those who could no longer fend for themselves should be terminated, rather than hinder the war effort. So it was that several military vehicles arrived at a facility ministering to the incapacitated. It was administered by a pastor, who met the officer in charge at the front entrance. "Pastor," the officer assured him, "you have done what you could for these, but it is now time for us to relieve you."

Knowing full well what this implied, the pastor resolutely replied: "If you harm these people God will damn you for eternity." At this, the officer paused momentarily, and then ordered his troops back into their vehicles. Thus, were these vulnerable people's lives preserved, at least for the time being.

William Watkins summarily contrasts a former absolute with a current one. As for the former, "Human life from conception to natural death is sacred and worthy of protection." As the latter, "Human life, which begins and ends when certain individuals or groups decide it does, is valuable as long as it is wanted."¹ Justice is defined accordingly.

In greater detail, I was conceived when my mother was past the time women generally give.birth Furthermore, she was not in the best of health. Even so, abortion was not a viable option. Although she had lingering adverse effects from the delivery, she was convinced that she had done *the right thing*.

More recently, a sexually active young couple were informed that the girl was pregnant. Her parents urged them to abort the fetus, rather than inhibit her education. Having reluctantly done so, they were plagued by grave misgivings. One thing led to another, so that their lives took a significant turn for the worse.

In still greater detail, "America's Judeo-Christian legacy is rooted in an ancient belief in the sanctity of all human life, including reborn life. This is founded on the biblical idea of the *imago dei*, image of God."² This *image* is said to represent, reflect, and reveal the invisible Lord God. It *represents* God especially in a stewardship capacity. Humans are charged with cultivating a wholesome environment, both from a functional and aesthetic perspective. Thus, the creation that was pronounced good is in significant measure preserved as a cherished legacy.

Conversely, humans are not meant to ravage their environment. This, in turn, recalls an imaginary account of two extra-terrestrials, as they approached the earth from outer space. Observing the contamination below, one concluded that humanity must be some form of contagion.

The *image* is also said to *reflect* the invisible Sovereign. This is especially associated with personal characteristics. In particular, the capacity to reason, to feel, and to deliberately act. For instance, humans can recall the past, anticipate the future, and choose among options.

This allows for a substantial divergence between God's ways and ours. In this regard, "As the heavens are higher than the earth, so are my ways higher than your ways and my thoughts then your thoughts" (Isa 55:8). In context, human finiteness is compounded by depravity.

Then, finally, the *image reveals* the Almighty. This appears associated primarily with ethical conduct. Humans have a profound sense of what is right and wrong, even though they differ in the particulars. As an

---

1. Watkins, *The New Absolutes*, 65.
2. Ibid., 67.

example, while what constitutes immodesty differs from one culture to the next, all cultures apparently share a concern for modesty.

If for no other reason, this should assure us of C. S. Lewis' sage counsel that we read one classic text for every contemporary one. This is guaranteed to broaden our horizons, and impress on us the complexity of life.

"Despite this pro-life heritage, today we are witnessing the removal of the right to life from various classes of people. The dislodging tools usually used are abortion, infanticide, euthanasia, population control and certain practices associated with genetic engineering."[3] Death is thus promoted as the solution to our problems, the panacea for our personal and social dilemmas.

Consider a classic case in point. Thomas Malthus (1766–1834) was an ordained Protestant minster, and a professor of economics and history. While he authored several works, he is best remembered for *An Essay on the Principle of Population*.

His central thesis was unambiguous. While the dominant view of his day insisted that an increase in population was desirable, he concluded an increase would further tax limited resources. Moreover, the greater the scarcity of food, the more poverty, sickness, and crime.

There were three notable means by which population might be curtailed. First, the occasion of premature death. This might occur from natural means—such as a famine, or from deliberate action—as with military conflict.

Second, by the reduction of the birth-rate. The appeal for *safe sex* comes to mind in this connection, although it is a misnomer—since promiscuous sex is never *safe*. Not with regard to birth control nor infectious disease. Then, in addition, select studies suggest that the program encourages greater sexual activity—offsetting any supposed benefit.

Finally, by way of moral restraint. The celibate life remains a viable option. This, in turn, recalls my brother—who never married. When mother would remind him that she would like to have grandchildren while still vigorous enough to enjoy them, he would reply: "I am looking for a girl who will support me in the way I hope to become accustomed."

It is a short step from Malthus' reasoning to the current values curriculum. The lifeboat analogy serves as a graphic example. In this con-

---

3. Ibid., 9.

nection, persons are cast afloat in an over-crowded lifeboat. We are thus encouraged to think that the world is seriously over-populated, if not currently than in the imminent future.

It remains to decide who will be cast overboard. An elderly man first draws our attention, since he has lived a full life. However, it is pointed out that as a research scientist he might make some discovery that would greatly benefit humanity. Instead, they decide to consider alternatives.

Clergymen do not as a rule fare well in the process. It appears that the service they render is not thought critical. Even so, they do better than some other professions—such as lawyers and used-car salesmen.

The point is that someone must be sacrificed for the greater good. If not to salvage the life of others, then to make it more amenable. The sanctity of life is thereby seriously compromised.

The theory of evolution has also had a largely negative impact on the sanctity of life. "Evolutionary theory swept through nineteenth-century America. Educators, scientists, moralists, politicians, ministers, journalist, people from every walk of life. For instance, American industrialists, often ruthlessly crushed competitors, citing natural selection as the law by which they operated."[4]

In the process, what was fashioned as a biological model came to be applied uncritically to political and social agendas. On the one hand, man's predatory nature was written off as a vestige from the past. On the other hand, utopian philosophies emerged to anticipate human progress.

Life can be terminated at any juncture: prior to birth, infanticide, whenever thought desirable, or during the declining years. It is estimated that every fifteen seconds the life of an unborn is aborted. Nearly a third of pregnancies are terminated in this manner. More than forty percent of women terminating a fetus have had at least one previous abortion. Partial birth abortion is an especially barbarous procure. More lives have been terminated by abortion since *Roe vs. Wade* than in all of the American military conflicts combined.

Infanticide was at one time a more prevalent option. It served a purpose not unlike abortion for convenience. It was not uncommon in the Roman Empire to leave infants by the wayside, either to perish or to be raised as prostitutes. Christians had a reputation for rescuing those cast aside, and raising them in a wholesome environment.

4. Ibid., 114.

While the Jewish holocaust stands out in our collective memory, it was preceded by the Armenian genocide. It was reported that when Adolph Hitler's associates cautioned him concerning international repercussions from his *final solution*, he cited the Armenian tragedy as indication of global apathy. As for the Jews, they had become a scapegoat for societies' ills.

Finally, there is euthanasia—implying a benevolent death. This has come to be applied to allowing nature to take its course, or by way of some coercive means. Moreover, the line between the two is often obscure. Consequently, efforts to govern the procedure often invite evasive action. This sometimes results from a concern to ease the suffering of the patient, lessen the burden to society, or some combination of the two.

We now turn to Jesus' life and ministry by way of celebrating life. He was raised in a culture where the sanctity of life was a given. The taking of life was limited to relatively rare occasions: as with capital punishment or in authorized warfare. Even then, precautions were taken to make certain that no injustice was involved.

Suicide was also discouraged. The rabbis reasoned that it would be preferable to endangering the lives of others, or dishonoring the Almighty. Seeing that life was perceived as a divine endowment, to repudiate it was considered an affront to the Giver.

Verbal assaults were viewed as depreciative of the integrity of another. As such, they were viewed as injurious to life. Accordingly, "A gentle answer turns away wrath, but a harsh word stirs up anger" (Prov 15:1).

The human disregard for the sanctity of life was ultimately traced to one's disposition (cf. Matt 5:22). One was already culpable, whether or not given the occasion, overtly to harm another. Then, too, the thoughts and intents of the heart are known to the Lord God.

Our attention is initially drawn to the announcement of Jesus' birth, "Glory to God in the highest, and on earth peace to men on whom his favor rests" (Luke 2:14). This constitutes *good news*, in that it affirms life in terms of fulfillment.

The term *shalom* conveys the notion of *peace* in the context of *well-being*. It is not simply the cessation of overt hostility, but the working of all things by God for those who are devoted to the Lord and persistent in their pious resolve. Not to be overlooked, this word was proclaimed to relatively non-observant folk—rather than to the meticulous religious establishment.

They named the child *Jesus*. "There were at least five High Priests who were called Jesus. In the works of the historian Josephus there appear about twenty people called Jesus, ten of whom were contemporary with our Lord."[5] While a common name, it admirably reflected the purpose of Jesus' mission—with the reminder that God is our deliverer.

His early life was succinctly characterized, "And Jesus grew in wisdom and stature, and in favor with God and man" (Luke 2:52). He matured, taking on adult ways. He exhibited *wisdom*, having to do with the skill of living. Both God and man took due notice. This portended good things from what would follow in the course of time.

Jesus was subsequently tempted in the wilderness. At one point, he observed: "It is written: 'Man does not live on bread alone'" (Luke 4:4; cf. Deut. 8:3). But rather in reflecting on God's word, as a means of spiritual sustenance.

He returned to Galilee *in the power of the Spirit*, and word spread concerning him throughout the countryside. He taught in their synagogues, and was well received by the populace. While the origin of the synagogue is uncertain, it is thought to have come into being during the exile. The term *synagogue* is derived from an assembly.

"The synagogue is one of the two centers of Jewish life. The home is the other. Through all the sacred texts of Judaism, the home and the family have been the heart of Jewish life."[6] It is by these means that prayer is nurtured, the scriptures expounded, and life nourished.

Jesus eventually made his way to Nazareth, where he was raised. Whereupon, he entered the synagogue—*as was his custom*. He was invited to read from the Isaiah scroll, and found the place where it was written: "The Spirit of the Lord is on me, because he has anointed me to preach good news for the poor. He has sent me to proclaim freedom for the prisoners and recovery of sight for the blind, to release the oppressed, to proclaim the acceptable year of the Lord" (Luke 4:18–19; cf. Isa 61:1–2). This contained Jubilee imagery crafted for the Messianic Age.

When he had finished, he handed the scroll back to the attendant, and sat down—in anticipation of giving instruction. The eyes of everyone fixed on him. He began by saying, "Today this scripture is fulfilled

---

5. Barclay, *Jesus As They Saw Him*, 10.
6. Robinson, *op.cit.*, 50.

in your hearing." This called for contrition, which was lacking in the congregation.

We next encounter "the first of some twenty-one miracles performed by Jesus in the Gospel of Luke. These miracles may be assigned to four basic categories: Exorcism, healings, resuscitations, and nature miracles."[7] Many maladies were attributed to demon possession. The symptoms were not necessarily different from those resulting from natural causes. The pertinent literature appears to single out the *aura of evil* as the most distinctive indicator. While difficult to put into words, it resembles an oppressive presence. These adversarial spirits were perceived as a dire threat to life, physical health, and spirituality.

Jesus' healings are far more numerous. As an example, when Simon's mother-in-law was suffering from a high fever, they asked Jesus to help her. "So he bent over her and rebuked the fever, and it left her. She got up at once and began to wait on them" (Luke 4:39). This brings to mind the saying, "One good deed deserves another."

Luke recalls two resuscitations: concerning a widow's son (7:11–12), and Jairus' daughter (8:40–42, 49–56). As for the former, Jesus was approaching the town of Nain, along with his disciples and a large number of persons. Whereupon, they met a similarly large gathering—accompanying a deceased person for burial.

He was the only son of a widowed mother. This brings to mind the rabbinic story concerning a similarly desperate person who sought out counsel. In response, the sage rabbi observed: "In so dire a situation only the Almighty can console and minister to your needs."

Jesus had compassion on the bereaved widow. He halted the procession. "Young man," he addressed the prone figure, "I say to you, get up!" At this, the deceased individual sat up and began to talk. Jesus then returned him to his mother.

All those present were filled with awe, and praised God. "A great prophet has appeared among us," they concluded. "God has come to help his people." As a result, word concerning Jesus spread even more rapidly.

As for nature miracles, one day Jesus urged his disciples: "Let's go over to the other side of the lake" (Luke 8:22). So they got into a boat, and set out. As they sailed, Jesus fell asleep. A squall came down on the lake, so that the boat became swamped. They were in considerable danger. In

---

7. Evans, *Luke*, 77.

this regard, the Sea of Galilee "lies 600 feet below sea level, and strong winds blowing through the deep gorges that feed into this basin often cause sudden and violent storms."[8]

The disciples awakened Jesus. ""Master, Master," they cried out, "we're going to drown!" He got to his feet, rebuked the wind and raging sea, and the storm subsided. All was calm, as before the storm.

"Where is your faith?" he inquired of them. It was as if to suggest that there was an inexplicable lapse brought on by the threatening circumstance. They, in turn, were amazed and wondered what sort of a person this was that "even the winds and the water obey him." Then, too, in contrast to the wavering faith of the disciples.

His public ministry would soon run its course. The cross loomed high on the horizon. Jesus took the Twelve aside, and confided in them: "We are going up to Jerusalem, and everything that is written in the prophets about the Son of Man will be fulfilled. (The Gentiles) will mock him, insult him, spit on him, flog him, and kill him. On the third day he will rise again" (Luke 18:31–33).

At every turn in the road, Jesus had affirmed life. Life as if it were a treasured gift; life as an investment in eternity; life as appreciatively shared with others—in the pursuit of justice. Accordingly, death was not a welcome prospect. Were there another way to achieve God's redemptive purpose, Jesus would have preferred the alternative. Even so, death did not have the final word. The report was shortly circulated, "He is risen!" This was coupled with the enthusiastic response, "He is risen indeed!"

---

8. Ibid., 133.

15

Justice and Idolatry

This chapter could be viewed as an extension of the previous one, in that idols are not living entities. It is understood that one could approach the topic from various perspectives. In this instance, I have chosen to delve into the matter concerning the exilic prophet Daniel and the medieval philosopher Maimonides.

Nothing is known of Daniel's early life except for the fact that he was born into a prominent family (cf. Dan 1:3). He was perhaps in his teens when taken into captivity. I imaginatively reconstructed this agonizing experience in an earlier context:

"The caravan had made its way up the slopes of the Trans-Jordan Plateau. From there it would travel along the King's Highway toward Damascus and eventually Babylon. The column paused long enough to look back toward Jerusalem. The torched city was billowing smoke into the air. Daniel, along with the other deportees, wondered what the future held with the temple in ruins and Jerusalem devastated."[1]

King Nebuchadnezzar subsequently instructed his chief court official Ashpenaz to select from among the Israelite *royal family and nobility* "young men without any physical defect, handsome, showing aptitude for every kind of learning, well informed, quick to understand, and qualified to serve in the king's palace" (Dan 1:4). They were to be instructed in the Babylonian language and literature.

---

1. Inch, *Scripture As Story*, 85.

The author does not protest their "study of polytheistic literature to which magic, sorcery, charms and astrology played a prominent part, though these had long been banned in Israel. These young men needed to be secure in their knowledge of Yahweh to study this literature objectively without allowing it to undermine their faith."[2]

Among those chosen were Daniel, Hananiah, Mishael, and Azariah. The official renamed them Beltshazzar, Shadrach, Meshach and Abednego. This would allow them to be more easily assimilated into the Babylonian culture.

There may, however, have been more at issue—since the selection of a name was thought to predispose a person in some way or another. This, in turn, recalls a time when one of the older West African students mentioned that he had petitioned his village elders to have his name changed. He concluded that this had resulted in his life taking a decided turn for the better.

While Daniel and his associates accepted Babylonian education and name, they asked to abstain from *the royal food and wine*. Not only might this violate the regulations regarding Hebrew diet, but also have religious connotations. "Why should he see you looking worse than the other young men your age?" the official protested. "The king would then have my head because of you."

"Please test your servants for ten days," Daniel pled. "Then compare our appearance with that of the young men who eat the royal food, and treat your servants in accordance with what you see." At the end of ten days, they looked healthier than those who ate from the king's table." We are thereby reminded of the fact that those who honor God, God honors in return (1 Sam 2:30).

When their training was completed, the Hebrews were brought before the king. After questioning them thoroughly, he concluded they were ten times more knowledgeable than all his wise men. *Ten times* appears idiomatic with reference to their manifest superiority (cf. Gen 31:41; Num 14:22).

In the second year of his reign, Nebuchadnezzar had a troublesome dream, but could not remember its content. Whereupon, he summoned his wise men to interpret the forgotten dream. "O king, live forever!" they saluted him. "Tell your servants the dream, and we will interpret it."

---

2. Baldwin, *Daniel*, 80.

Incidentally, the manner of interpreting dreams was passed down from one generation to the next, through select individuals. Something stood for something else, depending on its association with other ingredients.

"This is what I have firmly decided," the king resolutely replied, "if you do not tell me what my dream was and interpret it, I will have you cut into pieces and your houses turned into piles of rubble. But if you tell me the dream and explain it, you will receive from me gifts and reward and great honor."

Once again they pled, "let the king tell his servants the dream, and we will interpret it." Only then would their training be of any use.

"I am certain that you are trying to gain time," Nebuchadnezzar replied, "because you realize that this is what I have firmly decided." He wanted to leave no doubt concerning his intent.

"There is not a man on earth who can do what the king asks!" they bitterly complained. "No king, however great and mighty, has ever asked such a thing of any magician or enchanter or astrologer. No one can reveal it to the king except the gods, and they do not live among men." Here the themes of justice and idolatry are subtly combined to accent the unreasonable character of the request.

This made the king so angry that he ordered the execution of all the wise men of Babylon. It was his intent to include Daniel and his associates. "Why did the king issue such a harsh decree?" Daniel inquired. When the matter was explained to him, he offered to interpret the dream. During the night, the mystery was revealed to him in a vision. Then Daniel praised the *Lord of Heaven*, saying:

"Praise be the name of God for ever and ever; wisdom and power are his. He changes times and seasons; he sets up kings and deposes them. He gives wisdom to the wise and knowledge to the discerning. He reveals deep and hidden things; he knows what lies in darkness, and light dwells with him. I thank and praise you, O God of my fathers. You have given me wisdom and power, you have made known to me what we asked of you, you have made known to us the dream of the king."

Unlike the gods, who by common consent *do not dwell among men*, and are in fact non-entities.

I have found a man among the exiles from Judah who can tell the king what his dream means," Arioch the commander of king's guard confided. He seems disposed to take credit for the discovery.

"Are you able to tell me what I saw in my dream and interpret it?" Nebuchadnezzar asked for verification.

"No wise man, enchanter, magician or diviner can explain to the king the mystery he has asked about," Daniel allowed—being informed as to the means at their disposal, "but there is a God in heaven who reveals mysteries." Whereupon, he began by detailing the contents of the dream; which consisted of a large statue with a head of gold, chest and arms of silver, stomach and thighs of bronze, legs of iron, and feet a mixture of iron and baked clay. Then a rock was carved out, but not by human hands. It struck the statue, utterly demolishing it. "But the rock that struck the statue became a huge mountain and filled the whole earth."

Daniel then offered an interpretation: "You, O king, are the king of kings"—thus sovereign over all. After him, successive kingdoms would intervene. Then eventually "the God of heaven will set up a kingdom that will never be destroyed, nor will it be left to another people. It will crush all the kingdoms and bring them to an end, but it will endure forever."

Whereupon, the king prostrated himself before Daniel, and decreed that he be duly honored. "Surely your God is the God of gods and the Lord of kings and a revealer of mysteries," he concluded. Then Nebuchadnezzar placed Daniel in a high position, and lavished gifts on him. Moreover, at Daniel's request, he appointed Shadrach, Meshach, and Abednego as provincial administrators.

Perhaps inspired by the dream, the king subsequently made an idol of gold, ninety feet high and nine feet wide, and set in on the plain of Dura—in the province of Babylon. He then summoned a variety of public officials to be present at its dedication. Whereupon, the herald proclaimed: "This is what you are commanded to do, O peoples, nations and men of every language. As soon as you hear the sound of the horn, flute, zither, lyre, harp, pipes and all kinds of music, you must fall down and worship the image of gold that King Nebuchadnezzar has set up" (3:4). Otherwise, the person would be thrown into a blazing furnace.

As for apt commentary, "Babylon itself and its environs had become distinctly cosmopolitan. But the multiple listing of addresses is part of the art of the storyteller; so, too, is the constant repetition of them. By such means, and in keeping with ancient protocol, the preeminence of the king is demonstrated."[3]

---

3. Anderson, *Daniel: Signs and Wonders*, 31.

Certain of the astrologers subsequently reported that Daniel's associates had failed to comply with the decree. The king was furious, and summoned them to give an account of their behavior. "Is it true that you do not serve my gods or worship the image of gold I have set up?" he asked for confirmation. He then reminded them of the consequence of a failure to heed his injunction. "Then what god will be able to rescue you from my hand?" he rhetorically inquired.

Daniel's associates replied, "O Nebuchadnezzar, we do not.need to defend ourselves before you in this matter. If we are thrown into the blazing furnace, the God we serve is able to save us from it. But even if he does not, we want you to know, O king, that we will not serve your gods or worship the image of gold you have set up." Two of three things are certain. As for the former, they will not participate in idolatry, and God is able to deliver them. As for the latter, they do not presume to know whether he will do so on this occasion.

The king's fury again asserted itself. He commanded that the furnace heated *seven times hotter than usual*, and the offenders cast into it. He meant to make sure that they would not escape the ordeal. The flames were so hot that they reached out to engulf the guards.

"Look!" Nebuchadnezzar exclaimed in amazement. "I see four men walking around in the fire, unbound and unharmed, and the fourth looks like a son of the gods." Whereupon, he called Daniel's associates by name, as servants of the Most High God—a term reserved in polytheism as the supreme deity. "Come out!" he commanded them, "Come here!" At his bidding, they came forth. The officials crowded around them, and saw that they had not been injured.

Then the king declared: "Praise be the God of Shadrach, Meshach and Abednego, who has sent his angel and rescued his servants: They trust in him and defied the king's command and were willing to give up their lives rather than serve or worship any god except their own God." So it was that he decreed that any who would defame the God worshiped by Daniel's associates be executed—"for no other god can save in this way." He then promoted the three servants of the Most High God.

Here we take leave of the account of Daniel and his associates, while appreciatively recalling their resolute faith. Such had withstood the coercive idolatry with which they had to contend. As advocates of justice, and over against the caprice of the gods. Then as a lingering example to subsequent generations.

Maimonides next invites our attention. Moses ben Maimon was not only a towering figure in Judaism, but in medieval philosophy as well. He was born in Cordoba, Spain; the son of a well-to-do scholarly family. He was educated at first by his father, a rabbinic judge. He subsequently settled in Fez, Morocco—where he received training in medicine. Maimonides eventually moved to Cairo, and became the court physician, along with a highly respected leader of the sizable Jewish community.

In particular, we will focus on his *Thirteen Principles of the Jewish Faith*.[4] While these were composed early on, they set forth an agenda which would continue to dominate his considerable contribution. As such, they demonstrate the deliberate nature with which he set about to articulate his convictions.

1. *I believe with perfect faith that God is the Creator and Ruler of all things. He alone has made, does make, and will make all things.* The refrain *I believe with perfect faith* is by way of expressing a settled conviction. While indebted to reason, Maimonides does not feel restricted by it. As expressed by Augustine, "All truth is God's truth."

First among his settled convictions is that God is sovereign. As noted in an earlier context, he maximizes the good and minimizes the evil (cf. Exod 20:5–6). In more graphic imagery, he holds back the chaos that threatens to return. This is by way of resilient grace.

2. *I believe with a perfect faith that God is One. There is no unity that is in any way like His. He alone is our God—He was, He is, and He will be.* In the beginning, he existed in solitary splendor. He currently has no rivals. In the end, he alone will exercise righteous justice.

Unlike God, humans derive their identity from others. Their parents, and the generations that preceded them, even though each person draws in unique ways on his or her cultural legacy. So that unity in human terms resembles constructive diversity.

3. *I believe with perfect faith that God does not have a body. Physical concepts do not apply to Him. There is nothing whatsoever that resembles Him at all.* In this regard, Jesus affirmed: "God is spirit, and his worshipers must worship in spirit and in truth" (John 4:24). In this connection, he meant to point out that the critical thing is not *where* but *how* we worship.

---

4. Robinson, *op. cit.*, 416–417.

As pointed out in another context, God-talk is analogical. He has no actual hands at his disposal but ours. He is not for this reason less real, although not tangible. His is an awesome presence.

4. I believe with perfect faith that God is first and last. In this regard, "If the universe has been designed by God, then it must have a purpose. If that purpose is never achieved, God will have failed. If it is achieved, the continuation of the universe will be unnecessary. The universe, at least as we know it, will come to an end."[5]

If then we are without God, we are without hope. For this life or the one to come. For ourselves or for others we cherish. As the Russian novelist Fedor Dostoevski observed, "Either we worship God or the hole."

5. I believe with perfect faith that it is only proper to pray to God. One may not pray to anyone or anything else. Not to the spiritist, who reaches out to the departed. Not the scientist, who reflects on the nature of things. Not to some technique, meant to give us an advantage over others.

Now *prayer* is privileged communication. Accordingly, Jesus instructed his disciples to pray: "Our Father in heaven, hallowed be your name" (Matt 6:9). This before all else. Then "your kingdom come, your will be done on earth as it is in heaven." Thus without equivocation. After that, in still other regards.

6. I believe with perfect faith that all the words of the prophets are true. Including Moses, characterized by Maimonides as *the chief of the prophets*. Then, too, those who faithfully followed in his footsteps.

"Above all, you must understand that no prophecy of Scripture came about by the prophet's own interpretation. For prophecy never had its origin in the will of man, but men spoke from God as they were carried along by the Holy Spirit" (2 Pet 1:20–21). (Principles 7 and 8 are along a related line.)

9. I believe with perfect faith that this Torah will not be changed, and that there will never be another given by God. "Do not think that I have come to abolish the Law or the Prophets," Jesus cautioned; "I have not come to abolish them but to fulfill them" (Matt 5:17). That is, to bring them to fruition.

The rabbis debated in what sense the Torah was applicable to the righteous Gentile. There was a wide divergence of opinion. According

---

5. Davies, *God and the New Physics*, 199.

to a common saying, "Where there are two Jews, there are at least three distinct points of view.

10. *I believe with perfect faith that God knows all of men's deeds and thoughts.* It is thus written (Psa 33:15): "He has molded every heart together. He understands what each one does." With this in mind, we should not be quick to judge the intents of others. Nor should we overlook the fact that we have mixed motivations.

On a more positive note, even if our heart condemn us, God is greater than our misgivings. He shows compassion on the contrite, and lifts up those who have fallen by the wayside. He is slow to anger, and abounding in mercy.

11. *I believe with perfect faith that God rewards those who keep His commandments, and punishes those who transgress him.* In any case, God's justice is assured. This, rather than the severity of his judgment, ought to be our prime concern. Be assured that no one can con the Almighty.

It may not seem so at the present. It often appears that the godly suffer, while evil persons prosper. Even so, Maimonides remains convinced that things will eventually fall into place, in accord with the respective ways of the righteous and wicked.

12. *I believe in perfect faith in the coming of the Messiah. No matter how long it takes, I will await his coming every day.* Accordingly, Paul writes: "Now, brothers, about times and dates we do not need to write to you, for you know very well that the day of the Lord will come like a thief in the night" (1 Thess 5:12).

If like *a thief in the night*, then unexpectedly. People are carrying on as usual. Unlike the approach commended by the Jewish stalwart.

13. *I believe with perfect faith that the dead will be brought back to life when God wills it to happen.* As evidence that his agenda has been achieved. In spite of all the obstacles encountered, and resistance to his righteous initiatives.

So also according to his timetable. As C. S. Lewis reminds us, only he knows when more time will not serve any good purpose. Thus are we encouraged to live justly, and to avoid idolatry.

16

Justice and Reality

THE TERM *REALITY* IS EMPLOYED IN THIS CONTEXT AS ASSOCIATED WITH the actual circumstances, whether ideal or not. Initially, we are assured of God's existence. Not simply in some abstract sense, but dynamically active in his sovereign role. In this regard, "Yours, O Lord, is the kingdom; you are exalted as head over all. Wealth and honor come from you; you are the ruler of all things. In your hands are strength and power to exalt and give strength to all" (1 Chron 29:11–12).

The text appears at the critical juncture between the reigns of David and Solomon. Human kingdoms wax and wane, as allowed by divine providence. God nonetheless endures change, his authority undiminished. Consequently, "Righteousness exalts a nation, but sin is a disgrace to any people" (Prov 14:34).

This, in turn, recalls meeting an alert pre-school lad on the street. "God is here," he announced, motioning with his hand before him. I acknowledged his observation. "And God is there," he added—waving his hand behind him.

"You mean to say that God is everywhere," I concluded.

"Yes!" he emphatically declared. A broad grin graced his face, as he trudged confidently on down the street.

This also brings to mind Karl Barth's memorable appeal, "Let God be God." Do not relegate him to some secondary role. Accordingly, do not attempt to usurp his authority. As when we attempt to impose our preferences on others.

If God is God, then Peter Berger's graphic description of life as within a *sacred canopy* is not far off the mark. Life is essentially sacred, and so in all its particulars. This strikingly contrasts to the jungle code of survival of those most fit. Or as my maternal grandmother would say, "Each on his own, and the devil gets the hindmost."

In addition, both space and time can take on special significance. For instance, the Holy Land is especially revered by three major faiths: Judaism, Christianity, and Islam. As for Judaism, it is the promised land. Herein God would cultivate a chosen people, as a light to the Gentiles.

As for Christianity, it is the place of origin. God is no closer there than any place else, but there are vivid reminders of what transpired. Galilee especially in the springtime recalls Jesus inquiry: "And why do you worry about clothes? See how the lilies of the field grow. They do not labor or spin. Yet I tell you that not even Solomon in all his splendor was dressed like one of these" (Matt 6:28–29).

As for Islam, Jerusalem is said to have been the place where Mohammed was caught up into heaven. In any case, the region is associated with Muslim conquest.

As for special times: "The Jewish calendar is replete with holidays, each bearing its own distinctive historical and theological motif. The major festivals can be divided into two categories—the Pilgrim Holidays of Passover, Pentecost, and Tabernacles when Jews in ancient times would visit the temple in Jerusalem to celebrate, and the High Holy Days comprising Rosh Hashanah (New Year's Day) and Yom Kippur (Day of Atonement)."[1] There are also minor festivals and fast days. Both Christianity and Islam likewise observe special occasions.

Qualifications aside, life constitutes an extended celebration. Since God is good, and his ways are good. In Jewish tradition, this is recalled by a series of blessings. For instance, "Blessed are You Adonai our God, Ruler of the Universe, who brings forth bread from the earth." In addition, "Blessed are You Adonai our God, Ruler of the Universe, who makes the work of Creation." Finally: "Blessed are You Adonai our God, Ruler of the Universe, who makes the creatures different."[2]

The existence of God is largely a given in traditional cultures. In this connection, I was discussing the theistic arguments for God's existence

---

1. Eckstein, *op. cit.* 75.
2. Robinson, *op. cit.*, 20–21.

with my class of Nigerian students, when one of the young ladies raised her hand. "There doesn't seem to be any purpose in this," she protested, "since everyone believes in the existence of God." Instead, she felt our task was to assure persons that the High God had revealed himself in his Son. Incidentally, it was assumed that the veiled character of the father is subsequently revealed in his son.

While allowing that her point was well-taken, I pointed out that for many in Western Civilization this was no longer the case. In addition, this secular way of reasoning was making its way into the urban areas of West Africa. This seemed to her an incredible development.

The *Humanist Manifesto* served as a means for crystallizing secular thought. As expressed in the first of three such documents: "Humanism asserts that the nature of the universe depicted by modern science makes unacceptable any supernatural or cosmic guarantees of human values.... In the place of the old attitudes involved in worship and prayer the humanist finds his religious emotions expressed in a heightened sense of personal life and in a cooperative effort to promote social well-being."[3]

"The fool says in his heart, 'There is no God,'" the psalmist counters (14:1). In context, this does not pertain expressly to the theoretical but to the practical atheist. One may allow that God exists, but act as if he or she is not held accountable. Whether overtly religious or not, this is indeed folly.

Not only does God exist, but creation as well. Heaven and earth, light and darkness, the waters above and below, dry ground, vegetation, the greater and lesser lights, living creatures that negotiate the ground, water, and sky, and humans. These accommodate to one another under ideal circumstances, but may otherwise compete.

This recalls a conundrum from Philosophy 101: "How is one to know whether he is a human dreaming to be a butterfly, or a butterfly dreaming to be human?" In other words, what is the relationship between perception and reality? In any case, one is ill-advised to attempt to walk through a closed door. For all practical purposes, we assume that the world is substantial.

Moreover, nature serves as a tutor. "Do you not say, 'Four months more and then the harvest?'" Jesus inquired. "I tell you, open your eyes and look at the fields! They are ripe for harvest" (John 4:35). The agri-

---

3. *Humanist Manifest I*, Fifth and Ninth.

cultural year appears to have been "divided into six two-month periods, seedtime, winter, spring, harvest, summer and the time of extreme heat. Thus four months elapsed between the end of seedtime and the beginning of harvest."[4] This might well have given rise to a proverbial saying, to which Jesus responds. Whether in this or some other regard, he means that there is greater urgency than might be assumed.

He subsequently observed: "As long as it is day, we must do the work of him who sent me. Night is coming, when no one can work" (John 9:4). In an agricultural economy, this readily conveyed the importance of using the time available, while less in an urban environ.

Assuming the world is not a figment of our imagination, we learn in order to do. In particular, be aware of those in need. Whereupon, be available to them in their need. Then, too, encourage them to provide for themselves as this becomes feasible. Meanwhile, be patient with their efforts, and forgiving of their offences.

In that the world genuinely exists, we are also encouraged to become engaged in holistic ministry. Such as is concerned for one's physical, social, and spiritual well-being. Not limited to one to the exclusion of others, although there may be a division of responsibilities.

We likewise encounter suffering in the real world. In this regard, Paul reflects: "I consider that our present sufferings are not worth comparing with the glory that will be revealed in us" (Rom 8:18). If this world is to be viewed as "a 'closed system,' suffering is a harsh and final reality that can never be explained or transcended. But a Christian views the suffering of this life in a larger, world-transcending context . . . with the confident expectation that suffering is not the final world."[5]

In addition, it would seem that our capacity to experience joy is more or less commensurate with that of suffering. This is brought out in a story I have repeated on other occasions. It seems that a group of devout Jews were lamenting the destruction of their beloved temple, except for one—who seemed strangely pleased. "How can you rejoice at such a tragic event?" they inquired of him

If the destruction of the temple can produce such anguish," he observed, "imagine the rejoicing associated with its restoration."

---

4. Morris, *The Gospel According to John*, 246.
5. Moo, *op.cit.*, 511.

Justice and Reality

It remains to touch on some biblical examples that illustrate the subtle mixture of justice and reality. Now there was famine in the land, and Abram (Abraham) went down to Egypt "I know what a beautiful woman you are," he assured his wife Sarai. "When the Egyptians see you, they will say, 'This is his wife.' Then they will kill me but will let you live. Say you are my sister, so that I will be treated well for your sake and my life will be spared because of you" (Gen 12:13–14).

When the Egyptians officials saw her, they appreciatively reported her beauty to Pharaoh. Whereupon, she was escorted to his palace. Abraham was treated well for her sake, and "acquired sheep and cattle, male and female donkeys, menservants and maidservants, and camels." This was as he had anticipated.

However, the Lord was displeased, and inflicted Pharaoh and his household. At this, he protested: "Why did you say, 'She is my sister,' so that I took her to be my wife? Now go!" Then Abraham took his leave, along with his wife and possessions. "The wife/sister theme appears three times in Genesis. The logic is possible that if an individual in power desired to take a woman into his harem he might be inclined to negotiate with a brother, but he would be more likely to eliminate a husband."[6] It was, nonetheless, abhorrent from the divine perspective.

Abraham came up out of Egypt, along with his wife and all the possessions he had gathered, and his nephew Lot. Lot had also acquired considerable flocks and herds. As a result, there was quarreling between the herdsmen of Abraham and Lot.

This required a realistic appraisal of the situation. "Let's not have any quarreling between you and me, or between your herdsmen and mine, for we are brothers," Abraham urged. "Is not the whole land before you? Let's part company. If you go the left, I'll go the right; if you go to the right, I'll go to the left" (Gen 13:8–9). Initially, because there was room for all, providing they would divide it equitably.

Lot looked up, and saw that the whole plain of the Jordan was well watered, like the garden of the Lord, like the land of Egypt toward Zoar. This seemed preferable to him over the hill country of Judah. However, he had failed to factor in the evil behavior of those living in Sodom and Gomorrah.

---

6. Walton and Matthews, *op. cit.*, 37.

Thus, when the people of the region were subjected to a foreign alliance, Lot was carried away with the other prisoners. Upon hearing of the situation, Abraham set out to rescue him. Upon his return, Melchizedek, king of Salem and priest of God most High greeted him. "Blessed be Abram by God Most High, Creator of heaven and earth," the priest announced. "And blessed by God Most High, who delivered your enemies into your hand." Then Abraham gave him a tithe of everything he had recovered.

Later on, the patriarch interceded on behalf of the inhabitants of Sodom and Gomorrah. It was to no avail, since the situation had deteriorated beyond repair. Justice had to be served. "Hurry!" Lot was advised. "Take your wife and your two daughters who are here, or you will be swept away when the city is punished" (Gen 19:15). Thus, Lot and his daughters were saved, but his wife perished.

One day the older sister urged her younger sibling, "Let's get our father to drink wine and then lie with him and preserve our family line through our father" (19:32). This they did on successive nights, and each became pregnant. While this seemed a plausible way to proceed, it ignored the moral implications. As such, it would seem to suggest that they took on themselves the moral degradation of the people among whom they had lived. Then, too, it ignored the fact that God could provide in some acceptable manner.

The next episode increasingly illustrates the divergence between ancient and contemporary culture. Now Sarai, who had borne her husband no children, had an Egyptian maidservant named *Hagar*. Accordingly, she enjoined Abraham: "The Lord has kept me from having children. Go, sleep with my maidservant; perhaps I can build a family through her" (Gen 16:2). "The contrast between the two women is striking. Sarai was from the consummate lineage, free, brittle, aging, and barren. Hagar was a foreigner, a slave, resilient, young, and fertile."[7]

In a culture where *shame* plays a prominent role, Sarai's failure to birth a child was virtually intolerable. It was as if she had failed to fulfill her purpose in life. That she was not at fault was of relatively little consolation.

It was common practice for prominent women to have a maidservant. This was in keeping with their social status. Needless to say, some

---

7. Hartley, *op. cit.*, 164.

servants were better treated than others. Their situation could readily change, for better or for worse.

The ancients supposed that God granted fertility. In this regard, I have a miniature Baal in my collection, which was likely invoked for fertility purposes. In Jewish tradition, it is said that there are three involved in giving birth: God and the parents. It was thought that not only does God have invested interests, but also his claims take precedent.

Mesopotamian marriage contracts sometimes included the provision that the wife would engage a surrogate should she prove infertile. It would therefore appear that Sarai had ample precedent. It supposed that the servant would act on her behalf, and with her concurrence.

Abraham agreed. If the venture failed, there was nothing to be lost. Should it succeed, he would gain an heir.

Nevertheless, Sarai's proposal is cast in such a way as to recall her husband's previous suggestion that she pass herself off as his sister. She seems intent on not letting him forget his duplicity in the matter. This likely created lingering resentment, and friction between the couple.

Now Hagar conceived. This greatly enhanced her position in the family circle, causing her to depreciate her mistress. Then Sarai accosted her husband: "You are responsible for the wrong I am suffering. I put my servant in your arms, and now that she knows she is pregnant, she despises me. May the Lord judge between you and me." Particularly, because he had failed to reprimand the servant.

Sarai calls upon her husband to do the right thing, as indicative of divine justice. Should Abraham fail to take appropriate action, he will have to bear the consequences. In this regard, the psalmist inquires: "How long will you defend the unjust and show partiality to the wicked? Defend the cause of the weak and fatherless; maintain the rights of the poor and oppressed" (82:2–3).

"Your servant is in your hands," Abraham replied. "Do with her whatever you think best." Apart from his approval, she would not have been free to take action.

Then Sarai mistreated her servant, so that she fled from her. The angel of the Lord found her near a spring in the desert. "Hagar, servant of Sarai," the angel addressed her, "where have you come from, and where are you going?" This would imply that her rightful place was with her mistress.

It seems best to understand *the angel of the Lord* in generic terms, as synonymous with *messenger*. The angel thus speaks and acts on God's behalf. We are thus assured of his concern for the abused servant, her faults notwithstanding.

"I'm running away from my mistress Sarai," she replied. She did not choose to detail her grievances.

Then the angel enjoined her, "Go back to your mistress and submit to her." If that be construed as bad news, then as good news: "I will so increase your descendants that they will be too numerous to count." A large clan assured her of its prominence among the tribal people. So Hagar bore Abraham a son, who was named *Ishmael*.

The Lord God subsequently appeared to the patriarch. "I am God Almighty," he declared, "walk before me and be blameless. I will confirm my covenant between me and you and will greatly increase your numbers" (17:1–2).

Then Abraham prostrated himself before the Lord. "If only Ishmael might live under your blessing!" he exclaimed.

"Yes," the Almighty allowed, "but your wife Sarah (Sarai) will bear a son, and you will call him Isaac. I will establish my covenant with him as an everlasting covenant for his descendants after him. And as for Ishmael, I have heard you: I will surely bless him; I will make him fruitful and will greatly increase his numbers."

Now the Lord was gracious to Sarah, as he had said. She became pregnant and bore a son, whom they called *Isaac*. "God has brought me laughter, and everyone who hears about this will laugh with me," she reflected (21:6). Their laughter was associated with her giving birth at so advanced a time in life.

On the occasion of Isaac being weaned, Abraham held a great feast. However, when Sarah saw Ishmael mocking Isaac, she urged her husband: "Get rid of that slave woman and her son, for that slave woman's son will never share in the inheritance with my son Isaac."

While this displeased the patriarch, God confirmed that Isaac would be the legitimate heir. So it was that Hagar fled with Ishmael, and God intervened on their behalf. This was in keeping with his earlier promise to make him fruitful. Thus, justice copes with less than ideal situations.

17

INTERNATIONAL JUSTICE

"The proximity of Israel to the Mediterranean Sea and the Arabian Desert has greatly influenced topography, climate, flora, fauna, and human history. Throughout the ages, the desert and the sea have vied with one another for control of the land."[1] It is also situated between two great population centers of the ancient world: Mesopotamia and Egypt. It is for these reasons that the region has been graphically identified as *the land between*.

The former is expressive of the two ways: that of the righteous and that of the wicked. In this regard, "Blessed is the man who does not walk in the counsel of the wicked or stand in the way of sinners or sit in the seat of the mockers. But his delight is in the law of the Lord, and on his law he mediates day and night" (Psa 1:1–2).

"He is like a tree planted by streams of water, which yields his fruit." As when sustained by the moist climate generated from off the sea.

"Not so the wicked! They are like chaff that the wind blows away." This, in turn, recalls the hot dry air from off the desert.

This imagery is helpful as we come to explore the current topic. In this connection, it should be remembered that the Lord God is not simply the patron deity of a given people, but the sovereign Lord of all. Consequently, it should not come as a surprise that the prophets showed a concern for the peoples surrounding them. In other words, justice is without boundaries.

Amos serves as a prime example. Various literary forms comprise the text. "*Judgment speeches*, almost entirely poetic, are the backbone

---

1. Rasmussen, *NIV Atlas of the Bible*, 16.

of the book. They may be introduced by a 'messenger formula', usually include an accusation (or indictment) of sin and an announcement (or threat) of punishment . . . and may conclude with an oracle or closing messenger formula."[2]

Vision reports provide a second major component of the text (cf. 7:1–3, 4–6, 7–9; 8:1–2, 9:1–4). These maintain more of the veiled character of divine revelation than discourse as such. A more extensive list of literary forms includes biographical narrative (cf. 9:11–15), salvation promise (cf. 9:11–15), repetition (cf. 3:3–6), call to attention (cf. 3:1; 4:1), quotations (cf. 2:12; 4:1), responses to voiced opposition (cf. 2:1), punning (cf. 5:5), and gestures (cf. 4:12). Qualifications aside, it should be noted that the medium is the message.

Amos sets out to address the degenerate political, social, and religious life of the northern kingdom, although not to the exclusion of other regional entities. In this regard, a formal recognition of the Mosaic Covenant was not sufficient to restore vitality to the Israelite community. Instead, the populace had to come to grips with the spiritual demands of the covenant, lest their wickedness prevail.

The text falls into three major segments: the first containing several brief oracles concerning nearby nations (1:1—2:16), the second a collection of short addresses on the judgment of Israel (3:1—6:14), and the third a series of visions interspersed with biographical references to the prophet (7:1—9:15). We will focus our attention on the first of these segments, in terms of international justice.

It nonetheless serves to get a running start. "The words of Amos, one of the shepherds of Tekoa—what he saw concerning Israel two years before the earthquake, when Isaiah was king of Judah and Jeroboam son of Jehoash was king of Israel" (1:1). *Tekoa* was a small village located on a ridge ten miles due south of Jerusalem, dividing the cultivated land to the west from the wilderness of Judea to the east.

Amos was a shepherd by vocation, unlike the sanctuary prophets of the time. While his message was directed toward the northern kingdom, his residence in the south would make him still more suspect. Reference to *the earthquake* was a traditional way of identifying time, here associated with the reigns of the respective rulers of the two kingdoms. This, in

---

2. Hubbard, *Joel and Amos*, 102.

turn, recalls a village person who while not aware of his age, associated his birth with a notable flood.

Whereupon, the prophet announced: "The Lord roars from Zion and thunders from Jerusalem, the pastures of the shepherds dry up, and the top of Carmel withers" (1:2). "The lion was a fearful creature (cf. 3:8), whose roar is likened to the message of the prophet. *Zion* and *Jerusalem* are invoked by way of rebuke of the apostate shrines of the northern kingdom. They deviate from the faithful pattern cultivated in the City of the Great King."[3]

Several general observations are in order as we approach this initial portion of the text. First, the messenger formula serves to substantiate the prophet's credentials. These are not his words alone, but a divine oracle.

Second, evil practices ultimately constitute an offense against the Almighty. In creedal terms, sin is any lack of conformity to the will of God—whether in the form of commission or omission. It is set forth here in terms of international justice.

Third, the particular infractions are portrayed as inhumane. It appears that the nations are rebuked "not for idolatry nor false religions but for offenses commonly judged as evil by the prevalent standards of the day: cruelty to civilians in war (1:3, 13), selling of war prisoners into slavery (1:6, 9), violation of treaties (1:9, 11), and the mistreatment of a fallen king (2:1)."[4]

Fourth, this makes the nation exceedingly vulnerable. Vulnerable from the onslaught of its predatory neighbors. Vulnerable likewise from the moral erosion from within. Unable or unwilling to restrain themselves from wicked behavior, they cannot cope with adverse circumstances.

Fifth, the numerical pattern *for three sins, even for four* recalls wisdom literature (cf. Prov 30:18–19, 21–23, 29–31). The term *three* already implies repeated offenses, while the addition of *four* further accents their culpability.

Finally, it would appear that the accountability of any given people was proportionate to their familiarity with God's ways. Consequently, Judah's transgression is depicted in terms of its failure to respond to the school of the prophets. This is in keeping with the thesis that to the one to whom more is given, more is assuredly required (cf. Luke 12:48).

---

3. Inch, *Potpourri*, 121.
4. Hubbard, *Joel and Amos*, 136.

Damascus next draws the prophet's ire (1:3–5). "This is what the Lord says: 'For three sins of Damascus, even for four, I will not turn back my wrath. Because she threshed Gilead with sledges having iron teeth.'" *Sledges having iron teeth*, is likely a reference to the thoroughness with which Damascus subjected its victims, *Gilead* being singled out for mention.

The house of Hazael is subsequently mentioned, suggesting royal complicity in the matter. The populace of the city is also implicated, as can be seen from the breaking down of its gates. As was the surrounding area. Then, with a touch of irony, the exiles would return from whence they had come.

"God is portrayed as a judge who takes up the cause of the defenseless. In this role, he rebukes the haughty. He also consoles those who are oppressed. All things considered, he renders a righteous judgment."[5] It bears repeating, "Righteousness exalts a nation, but sin is a disgrace to any people" (Prov 14:34).

Philistia then solicits the prophet's rebuke (1:6–8). Four Philistine cities are mentioned: *Gaza*—southernmost and most prominent of the quartet, *Ashdod*—three miles inland, due west of Hebron, *Ashkelon*—located on the coast, and *Akron*—northernmost and nearest to Judah. Constricted to an area adjacent to the coastline, the Philistines expanded their influence into the Shephelah—a term derived from its unpretentious hills (as if bowed in prayer).

Slave-trade is singled out in the indictment. It appears to have been a calculated and extensive practice, rather than an occasional pursuit. For instance, "This is what the Lord says: 'For three sins of Gaza, even for four, I will not turn back my wrath. Because she took captive whole communities and sold them to Edom.'" Nor does this rule out other offenses, of which this would serve as a graphic example.

Tyre is faulted for a like offence (1:9–10). In greater detail, "This is what the Lord says: 'For three sins of Tyre, even for four, I will not turn back my wrath. Because she sold whole communities of captive to Edom, disregarding a treaty of brotherhood.'"

In the middle of the eighth century, Tyre, located on the Mediterranean coast just north of Ashur, was the leading city of Phoenicia. It was noted for its far-flung maritime trade. *The treaty of brotherhood* refers to some

---

5. Inch, *Potpourri*, 122.

political treaty, although details are lacking. Accordingly, honesty was considered a virtue, and was coupled with the exercise of justice.

Although *Edom* was mentioned earlier along with Philistia and Tyre, it is now singled out for criticism (1:11–12). There was a long history of hostility associated with Edom, said to have descended from Esau. This, in turn, recalls: "Esau held a grudge against Jacob because of the blessing his father had given him. He said to himself, 'The days of mourning for my father are near; then I will kill my brother Jacob'" (Gen 27:41). Although they were able to reach a reconciliation of sorts, there appears to have been lingering resentment cultivated from one generation to the next. There was, in fact, enough fault on both sides as to feed partisan resentment.

It came to pass that Moses sent word to the king of Edom, "This is what your brother Israel says: 'You know about all the hardships that have come upon us. Our forefathers went down into Egypt, and we lived there many years. The Egyptians mistreated us and our fathers, but when we cried out to the Lord, he heard our cry and sent an angel and brought us out of Egypt'" (Num. 20:14–16). This was calculated to solicit his sympathy for their former plight, and regard for God's intervention.

"Now we are here at Kadesh, a town on the edge of your territory. Please let us pass through your country. We will not go through any field or vineyard, or drink water from any well. We will travel along the king's highway and not turn to the right or to the left until we have passed through your property." Incidentally, *the king's highway* was a major trade route through the Trans-Jordan—accommodating general use.

But Edom replied, "You may not pass through here; if you try, we will march out and attack you with the sword." While not an idle threat; given the culture, the initial intent may have been to bargain.

The Israelites responded: "We will go along the main road, and if we or our livestock drink any of your water, we will pay for it. We only want to pass through on foot—nothing else." In this manner, to assure them that there is no hidden agenda.

Again they answered, "You may not pass through." Then Edom demonstrated its resolve by coming out against the Israelites with a formidable force. Whereupon, Israel turned away.

Then to compound its culpability, Edom took advantage of the Babylonian conquest to afflict the Israelites. In this connection, "Because you harbored an ancient hostility and delivered the Israelites to the sword at the time of their calamity, the time their punishment reached its climax, therefore as surely as I live, declares the sovereign Lord, I will give you over to bloodshed and it will pursue you" (Ezek 35:5–6).

In particular, the oracle declares: "For three sins of Edom, even for four, I will not turn back my wrath. Because he pursued his brother with a sword, stifling all compassion, because his anger raged continually and his fury flamed unchecked." Edom is thus judged "because it has never honored the bond of brotherhood. God watches over not only the relations between nations, but also who's within the circle of the family. No area of human life lies outside of God's (just) rule."[6]

Ammon now takes center-stage (1:13–15). "This is what the Lord says: 'For three sins of Ammon, even for four, I will not turn back my wrath. Because he ripped open the pregnant women of Gilead in order to extend his kingdom.'"

"In the periods when Israel was powerful, Ammon's territory was cramped between the Moabites to the south, the Israelites in Gilead on the west, Bashan on the north, and the great desert to the east. We cannot pin-point the specific campaign but we may assume it was coincident with the southern incursion of Damascus (cf. 1:3), the two ambitious states subjecting Gilead to a pincher's movement."[7]

The exchange of rule over disputed territory was calculated to intensify real and imagined grievances. While we may assume that neither party was altogether without reproach, Ammon is the target of the prophet's rebuke at this juncture. Israel would await its turn.

The assault on pregnant women might suggest indiscriminate slaughter. Otherwise, it was perhaps employed as a means of intimidation. In any case, God's displeasure is likened to a consuming fire.

Moab subsequently draws the oracle's attention (2:1–3). "This is what the Lord says: 'For three sins of Moab, even for four, I will not turn back my wrath. Because he burned, as if to lime, the bones of Edom's king.'" Moab lies east of the Dead Sea, and south of Ammon. Both are said to have descended from Lot's daughters, mentioned earlier concerning their intent to perpetuate their lineage by getting their father drunk and having sexual intercourse with him (cf. Gen 19:36–38). This would assuredly constitute a blemish on the family name.

---

6. Achtemeier, *op. cit.*, 182.
7. Hubbard, *Joel and Amos*, 136.

The desecration of the remains of a royal adversary was considered a serious breach of protocol (cf. 2 Kings 9:34). Such were entitled to a respectful burial. The failure to do so was thought utterly barbaric.

Moab would suffer defeat at the hands of its enemies, its ruler killed, along with his officials. In other words, any thought culpable. The rest would be implicated in less direct fashion, some more than others.

Judah does not escape unscathed (2:4–5). "This is what the Lord says: 'For three sins of Judah, even for four, I will not turn back my wrath. Because they have rejected the law of the Lord and have not kept his decrees, because they have been led astray by false gods, the gods their ancestors followed.'"

Only in this instance is the complaint explicitly religious in character. Judah has failed to keep its covenant commitment. Even though its offenses have not been as grievous as those associated with the northern kingdom, it is not without reproach.

Of course, its failure has profound social implications as well. As observed earlier, the rabbis were of the opinion that wickedness was spawned by idolatry. If one, then manifestly the other.

In greater detail, "Cursed is the man who dishonors his father and his mother. Then all the people shall say, 'Amen!'" (Deut 27:16). In still greater detail, "Cursed is the man who withholds justice from the alien, the fatherless or the widow. Then all the peoples shall say, 'Amen!'"

Israel is last on the prophet's list (2:6–16). This is what the Lord says: "For three sins of Israel, even for four, I will not turn back my wrath. They sell the righteous for silver, and the needy for a pair of sandals. They trample on the heads of the poor as upon the dust of the ground and deny justice to the oppressed. Father and son use the same girl and so profane my holy name. They lie down beside every altar on garments taken in pledge. In the house of their god they drink wine taken as fines."

This segment provides a transition to a more detailed elaboration of the guilt of the northern kingdom. Its polemic intent is obvious. As such, it is calculated to take issue with the more conciliatory appraisal forthcoming from the northern shrines. Also, it is not likely to enjoy the acclaim of the general populace.

Amos seizes on four critical concerns. First, selling the poverty-stricken into captivity. In particular, the *righteous*—who presumably have acted in good faith. In addition, for a paltry sum—indicating their demeaning approach to those less fortunate.

Second, perverting justice. In countless ways, but as a matter of course. Whenever it was thought convenient, without esthetical inhibitions. As a result, encouraging a similar kind of behavior in others.

Third, engaging in elicit sexual activity. In this representative instance, the father and son have sex with the same person. Then, in addition, giving rise to seemingly endless speculation. Such as in the case of the bloody-nose Pharisee, who was afraid to lust after an attractive woman, and so ran into a wall. This was meant to discourage a legalistic mentality.

Fourth, taking advantage of the destitute. In this regard, the *garments taken in pledge* would better serve to keep out the cold than provide comfort in the house of some pagan deity. In more general terms, persons were not to be denied the necessities of life, or the means of earning a livelihood.

"I destroyed the Amorite before them, though he was tall as the cedars and strong as the oaks." The term *Amorite* is a general designation, concerning those who lived in the land prior to the Israelite conquest. Although a formidable adversary, they had succumbed. Consequently, Israel should not expect preferential treatment.

"I brought you up out of Egypt, and I led you forty years in the desert, to give you the land of the Amorites." "God is also merciful, delivering the helpless and oppressed, and so Israel was delivered out of slavery in *Egypt* before it had one thing to deserve its redemption. The real God is faithful leading Israel through the terrors of the wilderness for *forty years*, despite its constant murmuring and rebellion."[8]

So are we reminded by the prophets, Amos being a prime example. As illustrated above, concerning international justice. If on former occasions, then in subsequent times as well. This serves a consolation to the righteous, and a warning to the wicked. In the latter regard, "Even the bravest warriors will flee naked on that day."

---

8. Achtemeier, *op. cit.*, 185.

18

The Legacy

THE TALE OF TWO KINGDOMS PERHAPS BEST ILLUSTRATES THE LEGACY of justice. The northern kingdom went into a deep spiral, from which there was no recovery. In contrast, the southern kingdom benefitted from periodic spiritual renewals, before eventually succumbing to the Babylonian incursion. Even then, the prophets held out hope for restoration. However, we first want to briefly consider the rise of the monarchy, and its subsequent division.

When Samuel was advanced in years, he appointed his sons judges for Israel. Nevertheless, they "did not walk in his ways. They turned aside after dishonest gain and accepted bribes and perverted justice" (1 Sam 8:3). This development was calculated to raise questions concerning the form of leadership in particular, and the wisdom of inherited leadership in general.

So all the tribal elders of Israel gathered, and came to Samuel at Ramah. "You are old, and your sons do not walk in your ways," they collectively observed; "now appoint a king to lead us, such as all the other nations have." It would appear that they were intent on rectifying the situation, that justice might be served.

Looking to all the other nations, however, gives the impression that they were inclined to take on the cultural pattern of the surrounding people, rather than seeking divine guidance. This resulted in an ambiguity that continued to plague the monarchy. On the one hand, "kingship could be seen as a rejection of God's own (rule), an unnecessary (and even unfortunate) intrusion into the relationship between God and his chosen people. On the other hand, it was a gift from God, a model and a channel through which God's relationship with Israel could be illustrated and strengthened."[1]

Samuel was displeased, and brought the matter before the Lord. "Listen to all that the people are saying to you," the Lord counseled him; "it is not you they have rejected, but they have rejected me as their king. As they have done from the day I brought them up out of Egypt until this day, forsaking me and serving other gods, so they are doing to you." Whereupon, the Lord instructed him to warn them of the burdens they would assume with a monarchy.

Saul had an impressive appearance, standing a head taller than all the rest. Accordingly, the populace readily acclaimed him as their ruler. He was followed by David, and then Solomon. Each of the three sovereigns started out well, but strayed from the Lord. David got better grades due in large measure to his contrite repentance.

Now Jeroboam was *a man of standing*, who was engaged in strengthening the fortification of Jerusalem. Upon leaving the city, he encountered the prophet Ahijah. The latter took the new cloak he was wearing, and tore it into twelve pieces. He then instructed Jeroboam to take ten pieces for himself. In this regard, the Lord revealed: "I am going to tear the kingdom out of Solomon's hand and give you ten tribes. But for the sake of my servant David and the city of Jerusalem, . . . he will have one tribe. I will do this because they have forsaken me and worshiped (pagan deities)" (1 Kgs 11:31–33). The *one tribe* was in fact made up of two: Judah and Benjamin, the former becoming the designation for the southern kingdom.

The two kingdoms would subsequently go their separate ways. While both drew upon a common heritage, each implemented it differently. This resulted in part from the different situations in which they found themselves, the northern kingdom being more vulnerable to alien influence. Then, too, the respective constituencies differed in the seriousness with which they approached their covenant commitment.

Jeroboam now fortified Shechem in the hill country of Ephraim, from which to rule the northern kingdom. He also erected golden calves at Bethel and Dan." It is too much for you to go up to Jerusalem," he reasoned. "Here are your gods, O Israel, who brought you up out of Egypt" (12:28). "Worshipers could see the bulls, and the animals themselves became objects of popular worship. While theoretically the people

---

1. Evans, *1 and 2 Samuel*, 41–42.

were still worshiping Yahweh, actually they were moving in the direction of Canaanite religion in which El and Baal were frequently likened to a bull."[2]

This had two results. First, it diminished the reliance of the northern kingdom on its southern counterpart. Second, it tended to assimilate the populace into the larger pagan culture surrounding them.

Now a man of God came from Judah to Bethel as Jeroboam was standing by the altar, intent on making an offering. "O altar, altar!" the visitor cried out. "This is what the Lord says: 'A son named Josiah will be born to the house of David. On you he will sacrifice the priests of the high places who now make offerings here, and human bones will be burned on you'" (13:2). As a sign, the altar would be split apart, and its ashes strewn around.

At this, the king motioned that he be seized, but his hand became shriveled. Moreover, the altar was split apart, and its ashes poured out. "Intercede with the Lord your God and pray for me that my hand may be restored," Jeroboam pled. The man of God acquiesced, having set the agenda for what would shortly transpire.

Meanwhile, Rehoboam reigned over the southern kingdom. The populace "set up for themselves high places, sacred shrines and Asherah poles on every high hill and under every spreading tree. There were even male shrine prostitutes in the land; the people engaged in all the detestable practices of the nations the Lord had driven out before the Israelites" (14:23–24).

In response to their defection, Shishak king of Egypt lay siege to Jerusalem. He carried off the treasures of the temple and royal palace. The splendor associated with Solomon's reign was thereby greatly reduced.

When Rehoboam was laid to rest, his son Abijah reigned in his stead. "He committed all the sins his father had done before him; his heart was not fully devoted to the Lord his God, as the heart of David his forefather had been" (15:3). Even so, the situation was not beyond recovery.

The fortunes of Judah now took a decided turn for the better. Asa ascended the throne, and "did what was right in the yes of the Lord, as his father David had done" (15:11). He expelled the male prostitutes, and got rid of all the idols his fathers had made. He even deposed his grandmother Mascah from her position as queen mother, because she had made a

---

2. Pfeiffer, *op. cit.*, 309.

repulsive Asherah pole. Although he did not go so far as to remove the high places, his heart was fully committed to the Lord.

Conflict with the northern kingdom continued unabated. This encouraged Asa to forge an alliance with Ben-Hadad of Damascus. This succeeded in causing Israel to withdraw its forces.

Nadab, son of Jeroboam, became king of Israel during the second year of Asa's reign in Judah. "He did evil in the eyes of the Lord, walking in the ways of his father and in his sins, which he caused Israel to commit" (15:26). It goes without saying that the ruler could have a pronounced influence on the populace.

Now Baasha plotted against and killed Nadab. As soon as he began to reign, he executed Jeroboam's *whole family.* This was by way of consolidating his rule. Moreover, "he did evil in the eyes of the Lord, walking in the ways of Jeroboam, and in his sin, which he caused Israel to commit" (15:34).

Accordingly, the Lord sent word: "I lifted you up from the dust and made you leader of my people Israel, but you walked in the ways of Jeroboam and caused my people Israel to sin and to provoke me to anger by their sins" (16:2). In this regard, what a person sows, he or she can expect to reap (cf. Gal. 6:7).

Elah now succeeded Baasha as ruler of Israel. Zimri, one of his officials, plotted against and killed him. Once he was enthroned, he executed Baasha's male relatives and friends. Again, this was for the purpose of consolidating his rule, without regard for the violation of justice.

Nonetheless, Zimri's reign was cut short. When it became known that he had murdered Baasha, the military declared their commander Omri his replacement. When Zimri realized his cause was lost, he retired to the citadel of the palace, and set it on fire. "So he died, because of the sins he had committed, doing evil in the ways of Jeroboam and in the sin he had committed and caused Israel to commit" (16:18–19).

A power struggle ensued. Some supported Tibni, while others promoted Omri. However, Omri's followers prevailed. He bought the hill of Samaria, which would serve as the capital of the northern kingdom. He, however, "did evil in the eyes of the Lord and sinned more than all those before him" (16:25). "His life as king, too, is simply subsumed under the heading 'idolater.' He took the throne; he sinned; he died."[3]

---

3. Proven, *1 and 2 Kings,* 129.

Omri's son Ahab succeeded him. He reigned in Samaria twenty-two years, and "Did more evil in the eyes of the Lord than any of those before him" (16:30). In this connection, he married Jezebel, daughter of Ethbaal king of the Sidonians, and devoted himself to Baal. Conversely, the worship of Yahweh was brutally repressed.

"It is in the context of Ahab's reign that we are introduced to one of the most colorful of the Biblical characters—Elijah. His name means *My God is the Lord*, an apt designation for so stalwart an opponent of Baalism."[4] He began his public ministry with the announcement of a drought, as a graphic way of expressing God's displeasure. He then hid himself in a ravine on the east bank of the Jordan River, where God provided for his need. When the brook dried up, a widow shared her scanty resources with him, and was rewarded with a miraculous provision that was not depleted. Sometime later, her son was restored to health.

Ahab had attempted without success to find the troublesome prophet. Now God instructed Elijah to announce that the drought would soon cease. "Is that you, you troubler of Israel?" the ruler inquired (17:16).

"I have not made trouble for Israel," Elijah protested. "But you and your father's family have. You have abandoned the Lord's commands and have followed the Baals. Now summon the people from all over Israel to meet me on Mount Carmel." Along with the four hundred and fifty prophets of Baal, and the four hundred prophets of Asherah—sponsored by Jezebel.

When the people had assembled, Elijah inquired of them: "How long will you waver between two opinions? If the Lord is God, follow him; but if Baal is God, follow him." There was no response. Then the prophet proposed that two altars be prepared, and the respective deities invoked. With the intent that the "god who answers by fire—he is God." The people agreed.

Therefore, the prophets prepared their sacrifice, and called on the name of Baal from morning until noon. Whereupon, Elijah began to taunt them. "Shout louder!" he urged. "Perhaps he is deep in thought, or busy, or traveling. Maybe he is sleeping and must be awakened." So they shouted louder, and slashed themselves in religious frenzy. Thus they persisted until it was time for the evening sacrifice. At which, the narra-

---

4. Inch, *Scripture As Story*, 76.

tor observes: "But there was no response, no one answered, no one paid attention."

Then Elijah summoned the people to gather around him. He rebuilt the altar to Yahweh, which was in ruins. He arranged the wood, cut the bull into pieces, and laid it on the altar. Then he instructed those standing by to fill four large jars with water and pour it on the offering. "Do it again," he said. "Do it a third time." By now the water had not only soaked the altar, but run down into the trench surrounding it.

Coinciding with the time of the evening sacrifice, the prophet petitioned: "O Lord, God of Abraham, Isaac and Israel, let it be known today that you are God in Israel and that I am your servant and have done all these things at your command." Then the fire of the Lord consumed all in sight. Whereupon, the people cried out: "The Lord—he is God! The Lord—he is God!" Thus, Elijah attempted to draw Israel back from the brink of disaster.

Meanwhile, there were mixed reports from Judah. Jehoshaphat ascended the throne in the fourth year of Ahab's reign over Israel. "In everything he walked in the ways of his father Asa and did not stray from them. The high places, however, were not removed, and the people continued to offer sacrifices and burn incense there" (22:43).

Ahaziah, son of Ahab, subsequently became king of Israel. "He did evil in the eyes of the Lord, because he walked in the ways of his father and mother and in the ways of Jeroboam, who caused Israel to sin. He served and worshiped Baal and provoked the Lord, the God of Israel, to anger, just as his father had done" (22:52–53). Since Ahaziah had no son, Joram succeeded him.

The ninth century ended on a downbeat. Baalism, after permeating Israel and impacting on Judah, left both kingdoms in a greatly weakened condition. The Syrian king Hazael employed this situation to extend his influence throughout the region.

A flurry of prophetic activity inaugurated the eighth century, primarily associated with the northern kingdom. "With little exception, Israel would remain impervious to the pleas of the prophets. It plunged headlong into destruction eventuating in the fall of Samaria in 722 B.C. to the Assyrians. The populace was resettled, and largely assimilated.

Meanwhile, the fortunes of Judah continued to vacillate. Hezekiah ascended the throne. He was twenty-five years of age at the time, and reigned for twenty-nine years. "He did what was right in the eyes of the

Lord, just as his father David had done. He removed the high places, smashed the sacred stones and cut down the Asherah poles" (2 Kings 18:3–4). He also destroyed the bronze snake Moses had made, since it was being employed for religious purposes.

Accordingly, "Hezekiah trusted in the Lord, the God of Israel. There was no one like him among all the kings of Judah, either before or after him. He held fast to the Lord and did not cease to follow him; he kept the commands the Lord had given Moses." As a result, he enjoyed great success.

When threatened by the Assyrians, Hezekiah pled: "Now, O Lord our God, deliver us from his hand, so that all kingdoms on earth may know that you alone, O Lord, are God" (19:19). That night the angel of the Lord devastated the Assyrian forces, so that when they arose the next morning *there were all the dead bodies*! "So Sennacherib king of Assyria broke camp and withdrew. He returned to Ninevah and stayed there."

Both kings who preceded Josiah (Manasseh and Amon) did evil in the eyes of the Lord. As for the former, he "rebuilt the high places his father Hezekiah had destroyed; he also erected altars to Baal and made an Asherah pole as Ahab king of Israel had done. In both courts of the temple of the Lord, he built altars to all the starry hosts" (21:3, 5). In addition, he sacrificed his own son in the fire, practiced sorcery and divination, and consulted mediums and spiritists.

As for the latter, he "walked in all the ways of his father; he worshiped the idols his father had worshiped, and bowed down to them. He forsook the Lord, the God of his fathers, and did not walk in the ways of the Lord" (21:21–22). As on previous occasions, this recalls the ways of the righteous and wicked—as depicted by the psalmist (cf. Psa 1).

Now Josiah was only eight years of age when he ascended the throne, and he reigned for thirty-one years. In the eighteenth year of his reign, the *Book of the Law* was discovered in the temple precincts. "Only then does he comprehend just how far short of divine acceptance Judean worship falls. As soon as he was aware of the contents of the book, he acted as a pious king should. He tore his *robes* in grief and despair and sent various of his officials to *inquire of the Lord*."[5]

Whereupon, Josiah determined to renew the covenant with his people. Accordingly, "to follow the Lord and keep his commands, regula-

---

5. Proven, *op/cit.*, 270–271.

tions and decrees with all his heart and with all his soul, thus confirming the words of the covenant written in this book" (23:3). Then all the people pledged themselves to abide by its stipulations.

In keeping with the renewal of the covenant, Josiah mandated that all the articles associated with the worship of Baal, Asherah, and the starry host be removed from the temple precinct, and had them burnt in the Kidron Valley. He also did away with the pagan priests appointed by the kings to burn incense on the high places. He likewise tore down the quarters of the male shrine prostitutes, which were in the temple precincts, and where women did weaving for Asherah. In these and other ways, he took a determined stand against invested pagan interests.

"Neither before nor after Josiah was there a king like him who turned to the Lord as he did—with all his heart and with all his soul and with all his strength, in accordance with all the Law of Moses." Only Hezekiah is recalled in similarly glowing terms, as exemplary sovereigns. "To love God, then, *with all your heart and with all your soul*, meant with the whole self, including your rationality, mental capacity, moral choices and will, inner feelings and desires, and the deepest roots of your life."[6] Josiah alone is explicitly mentioned as measuring up to this standard (cf. Deut 6:5).

"Nevertheless, the Lord did not turn away from the heat of his fierce anger, which burned against Judah because of all Manasseh had done to provoke him to anger. So the Lord said, 'I will remove Judah also from my presence as I removed Israel'" (23:26–27). So it came to pass that Nebuchadnezzar lay siege to Jerusalem.

"*Lamentations* was composed as a funeral dirge upon the destruction of Jerusalem. It describes the cruelty of the plundering invaders, the ravages that attend plague and famine, the helpless of the inhabitants, and the utter ruin of the city. It likewise illustrates how religious idealism flounders with the hard realities of life."[7]

Thus the legacy of justice ran its course concerning two kingdoms. As for Israel, it suffered throughout the succeeding reigns. As for Judah, periodic revivals postponed the day of reckoning, and cultivated hope in the return from exile. Then, in the long run, justice would triumph with the Messianic Age.

---

6. Wright, *op. cit.*, 99.
7. Inch, *Scripture As Story*. 83.

Bibliography

Achtemeier, Elizabeth. *Minor Prophets I*. Peabody, MA: Hendrickson, 2002.
Ackerman, Bruce. *Social Justice in a Liberal Society*. New Haven, CT: Yale University, 1980.
Anderson, Hugh, editor. *Jesus: Great Lives Observed*. Englewood Cliffs, NJ: Prentice-Hall, 1967.
Anderson, Robert. *Daniel: Signs and Wonders*. Grand Rapids: Eerdmans, 1984.
The Apology of Aristides. In Anti-Nicene Fathers, vol. 9, edited by A. Cleveland Coxe, 258–77.
Baldwin, Joyce. *Daniel*. Downers Grove, IL: Inter-Varsity, 1978.
Barclay, William. *Jesus As They Saw Him*. New York: Harper & Row, 1962.
Bauman, Michael. "The Dangerous Samaritans: How We Unintentionally Injure the Poor." In *God & Caesar*, edited by Michael Baumann and Daniel Hall, 201–15. Camp Hill, PA: Christian Publications, 1994.
Bauman, Michael, and Daniel Hall, editors. *God & Caesar*. Camp Hill, PA: Christian Publications, 1994.
Bellinger, W. H., Jr. *Leviticus, Numbers*. Peabody, MA: Hendrickson, 2005.
Bingham, D. Jeffrey. "Irenaeus and the Kingdoms of the World." In *God & Caesar*, edited by Michael Bauman and Daniel Hall, 27–40. Camp Hill, PA: Christian Publications, 1994.
Bishops Letter. In *Six Theories of Justice*, authored by Karen Lubacqz, 71–74, Minneapolis, MN: Augsburg, 1986.
Broyles, Craig. *Psalms*. Peabody, MA: Hendrickson, 2005.
Bruce, F. F. *The Epistle to the Hebrews*. Grand Rapids: Eerdmans, 1990.
———. *Philippians*. Peabody, MA: Hendrickson, 1993.
Brueggemann, Walter. *Living Toward a Vision*. Philadelphia: United Church, 1976.
Carter, James. *John*. Nashville: Broadman, 1984.
Clement of Alexandria. *The Instructor*. In *Anti-Nicene Fathers*, vol. 2, edited by A. Cleveland Coxe, 208–96.
Clorfene, Chaim and Yakov Rogalsky. *The Path of the Righteous Gentile*. Southfield, MI: Targum, 1987.
Cole, R. Alan. *Exodus*. Downers Grove, IL: Inter-Varsity, 1973.
Coxe, A. Cleveland (ed.). *Anti-Nicene Fathers*, 10 vols., Peabody, MA: Hendrickson, 1994.
Davies, Paul. *God & the New Physics*. New York: Simon & Schuster, 1984.
Eckstein, Yechiel. *How Firm a Foundation*. Brewster, MA: Paraclete, 1997.

Estes, Daniel. "Psalm 100 and the Ethos of Political Leadership." In *God & Caesar*, edited by Michael Bauman and Daniel Hall, 7–25. Camp Hill, PA: Christian Publications, 1994.
Evans, Craig. *Luke*. Peabody, MA: Hendrickson, 1990.
Evans, Mary. *1 and 2 Samuel*. Peabody, MA: Hendrickson, 2003.
Forni, P. M. *Choosing Civility*. New York: St. Martin's Griffin, 2007.
Goldingay, John. *Isaiah*. Peabody, MA: Hendrickson, 2001.
Hagner, Donald. *Matthew 11–28*. Dallas: Word, 1995.
Hamilin, E. John. *Judges: At Risk in the Promised Land*. Grand Rapids: Eerdmans, 1983.
Hare, Douglas. *Matthew*. Louisville: John Knox, 1993.
Haring, Bernard. *The Law of Christ*, 3 vols. Westminster, MD: Newman, 1963.
Harris, J., C. Brown, and M. Moore. *Joshua, Judges, Ruth*. Peabody, MA: Hendrickson, 2003.
Harrison, R. K. *Jeremiah and Lamentations*. Downers Grove, IL: Inter-Varsity, 1973.
Hartley, John. *Genesis*. Peabody, MA: Hendrickson, 2003.
Heschel, Abraham. *The Prophets*. Peabody, MA: Prince, 2001.
Hoffmeier, James, editor. *Abortion: A Christian Understanding and Response*. Grand Rapids: Baker, 1987.
———. "Abortion and the Old Testament Law," *Abortion* (Hoffmeier, ed.). 49–63.
Hubbard, David. *Hosea*. Downers Grove: Inter-Varsity, 1989.
———. *Joel & Amos*. Downers Grove: Inter-Varsity, 1989.
Humanist Manifesto I. Online by way of the American Humanist Association.
Ignatius. *To the Trallians*. In *Anti-Nicene Fathers*, vol. 1, edited by A. Cleveland Coxe, 66–78.
Inch, Morris. *Exhortations of Jesus According to Matthew* and *Up From the Depths: Mark as Tragedy*. Lanham, MD: University Press of America, 1997.
———. *Potpourri: Common Sense & the Conspiracies, Covenant Echoes, & Amos Still Speaks*, New York: iUniverse, 2008.
———. *Saga of the Spirit*. Grand Rapids: Baker, 1985.
———. *Scripture As Story*. Lanham, MD: University Press of America, 2000.
———. *Understanding Bible Prophecy*. New York: Harper & Row, 1977.
———. *Why Take the Bible Seriously?* Baltimore: AmErica, 2001.
Keener, Craig. *Bible Background Commentary: New Testament*. Downers Grove, IL: InterVarsity, 1993.
Kline, Meredith. *Treaty of the Great King*. Grand Rapids: Eerdmans, 1963.
Lebacqz, Karen. *Six Theories of Justice*. Minneapolis: Augsburg, 1986.
Letter to Diognetus. In *Anti-Nicene Fathers*, vol. 3, edited by A. Cleveland Coxe, 23–36.
Lewis, C. S. *Mere Christianity*. London: Collins, 1961.
Marshall, I. Howard. *The Epistles of John*. Grand Rapids: Eerdmans, 1978.
Matthews, M. R. "The Implications of Western Theologies of Development for Third World Countries and Churches," *Evangelicals and Development* (Sider, ed.), 89–101.
Monsma, Stephen. *Positive Neutrality*. Grand Rapids: Baker, 1993.
Montefiori, C. G. "Jesus and the Rabbis." In *Jesus: Great Lives Observed*, edited by Hugh Anderson 155–57. Englewood Cliffs, NJ: Prentice-Hall, 1967.
Moo, Douglas. *The Epistle to the Romans*. Grand Rapids: Eerdmans, 1996.
Morris, Leon. *1 Corinthians*. Downers Grove, IL: Inter-Varsity, 1990.
———. *The Gospel According to John*. Grand Rapids: Eerdmans, 1995.
Mounce, Robert. *The Book of Revelations*. Grand Rapids: Eerdmans, 1977.

———. *Matthew*. Peabody, MA: Hendrickson, 1991.
Murphy, R., and E. Huwiler. *Proverbs, Ecclesiastes, Song of Songs*. Peabody, MA: Hendrickson, 1999.
Pfeiffer, Charles. *Old Testament History*. Grand Rapids: Baker, 1973.
Prager, Dennis, and Joseph Telushkin. *Why the Jews?* New York: Touchstone, 1965.
Proven, Iain. *1 and 2 Kings*. Peabody, MA: Hendrickson, 2003.
Rasmussen, Carl. *NIV Atlas of the Bible*. Grand Rapids: Zondervan, 1989.
Robinson, George. *Essential Judaism*. New York: Pocket, 2000.
Ryken, Leland, James Wilhoit, and Tremper Longman III, editors. *Dictionary of Biblical Imagery*. Downers Grove, IL: InterVarsity, 1998.
Sider, Ronald, editor. *Evangelicals and Development*. Philadelphia: Westminster, 1981.
Tertullian. *The Apology*. In *Anti-Nicene Fathers*, vol. 3, edited by A. Cleveland Coxe, 17–55.
Theissen, Gerd. *Sociology of Early Palestinian Christianity*. Philadelphia: Fortress, 1978.
Wall, Robert. *Revelation*. Peabody, MA: Hendrickson, 1991.
Walton, John, and Victor Matthews. *Bible Background Commentary: Genesis–Deuteronomy*. Downers Grove, IL: InterVarsity, 1997.
Watkins, William. *The New Absolutes*. Minneapolis: Bethany, 1996.
Wright, Christopher. *Deuteronomy*. Peabody, MA: Hendrickson, 1996.